Content

CHAPTER 1: THE POWER OF EARLY EDUCATION

CHAPTER 2: ADVANTAGES OF AI EDUCATION

CHAPTER 3: ADDRESSING THE DIVERSITY GAP IN TECH

CHAPTER 4: FOSTERING DIGITAL CONFIDENCE

CHAPTER 5: NAVIGATING ETHICAL AND SOCIAL IMPLICATIONS

CHAPTER 6: INSPIRING FUTURE AI LEADERS

CHAPTER 7: OVERCOMING CHALLENGES AND LOOKING AHEAD

CONCLUSION

Key Points Discussed Throughout the Book Regarding AI Education for Black Children
Reinforce the Importance of Early AI Education for Black Children's Development
Take Action by Supporting AI Education Initiatives and Advocating for Diversity in Tech
An Optimistic Outlook on the Positive Changes That Widespread AI Education for Black Children Can Bring to Society

INTRODUCTION

The Concept of Teaching AI to Black Children at an Early Age

In today's rapidly advancing technological landscape, the importance of equipping all children with a comprehensive understanding of artificial intelligence (AI) cannot be overstated.

However, there exists a pressing need to explore ways in which AI education can be effectively introduced to black children at an early age.

This section aims to delve into the significance of teaching AI concepts to black children and elucidate the benefits that early AI education can bring.

Additionally, it seeks to debunk common misconceptions about AI specifically tailored for young black minds and provide strategies for empowering them through this form of education.

Key Takeaways

- Equitable access to AI education bridges the digital divide and reduces disparities in education and professional realms.
- Teaching AI to black children enables them to create innovative solutions for real-world problems.
- Early AI education empowers black children with knowledge and skills for future success.
- Introducing AI concepts at an early stage promotes innovation and creativity among black children.

The Importance of Teaching AI to Black Children

The significance of instructing artificial intelligence (AI) to young black individuals resides in its potential to foster equitable access, technological empowerment, and future career opportunities.

By introducing AI education at an early age, black children can develop the necessary skills and knowledge to navigate the digital landscape and actively participate in the technological advancements shaping our society.

Equitable access is a pressing concern in today's increasingly digitized world. AI education can bridge the digital divide by providing equal opportunities for all students, including those from marginalized communities. By equipping young black individuals with AI literacy, we empower them to engage with technology on an equal footing and potentially reduce disparities that exist within educational and professional realms.

Moreover, teaching AI to black children can lead to technological empowerment. As they learn about AI algorithms, machine learning principles, and data analysis techniques, these young learners gain agency over their own technology use. This empowers them to not only consume but also create innovative solutions that address real-world problems faced by their communities.

Lastly, introducing AI education at an early age opens up future career opportunities for young black individuals. With the rapid advancement of technology in various sectors such as healthcare, finance, and transportation, there is a growing demand for professionals skilled in AI-related fields. Equipping black children with foundational knowledge of AI sets them on a path towards pursuing careers in these emerging fields.

Exploring the Benefits of Early AI Education for Black Children

To understand the potential advantages of introducing artificial intelligence education to young children from the black community, it is important to explore the benefits that such early exposure can offer.

- **Fosters a sense of belonging**: By providing AI education at an early age, black children can develop a sense of belonging in a field that has historically been dominated by other racial and ethnic groups. This exposure helps them feel included and valued in the technology sector.
- **Empowers with knowledge**: Early AI education equips black children with valuable knowledge and skills needed for future success. It empowers them to understand and navigate the increasingly AI-driven world, opening doors to diverse career opportunities.
- **Promotes innovation and creativity**: Introducing AI concepts at an early stage encourages innovative thinking among black children, enabling them to actively participate in shaping the technology's future development. This fosters creativity and problem-solving abilities critical for their personal growth.

Breaking Down Misconceptions about AI for Young Black Minds

Breaking down misconceptions surrounding artificial intelligence can have a transformative impact on the mindset of young minds from the black community. By dispelling myths and misunderstandings about AI, we can create an inclusive environment that fosters a sense of belonging for these children.

One common misconception is that AI is only for highly skilled individuals or those from privileged backgrounds. However, this notion fails to acknowledge the potential of AI as a tool for empowerment and social change. Educating young black minds about the possibilities of AI can help them see it as a field where they can excel and make meaningful contributions.

Another misconception related to AI is the fear that it will replace human jobs, particularly in marginalized communities. By highlighting the collaborative nature of AI and its ability to augment human capabilities rather than replace them, we can alleviate these concerns. It is important to emphasize that AI has the potential to create new job opportunities and increase efficiency across various sectors.

Furthermore, addressing misconceptions surrounding bias in AI algorithms is crucial in empowering young black minds. By acknowledging existing biases within AI systems and promoting transparency in their development, we can encourage critical thinking and active engagement with technology among these children.

Strategies for Introducing AI Concepts to Black Children at an Early Age

Implementing strategies that facilitate the understanding of artificial intelligence among young individuals from the black community is crucial for their early exposure to this field. By introducing AI concepts at an early age, we can empower black children and provide them with a sense of belonging in the rapidly evolving technological world.

To evoke emotion in our audience, we can highlight the following sub-lists:

- **Increased Representation**: Ensuring that black children see themselves reflected in AI-related materials such as books, toys, and media will foster a sense of belonging and inspire them to pursue careers in this field.
- **Culturally Relevant Content**: Developing AI educational resources that incorporate elements of African and African American culture will help black children connect with the subject matter on a deeper level, fostering a stronger interest and engagement.
- **Community Engagement**: Establishing partnerships between schools, community organizations, and AI professionals can create mentorship opportunities for black children. This interaction provides role models who share similar backgrounds and experiences, reinforcing their sense of belonging within the AI community.

Empowering Black Children through AI Education

A comprehensive approach to fostering inclusivity in AI education necessitates the empowerment of young individuals from underrepresented communities. In particular, empowering Black children through AI education is essential for promoting diversity and equity within this field. By providing Black children with access to AI education at an early age, they can gain valuable knowledge and skills that will contribute to their personal growth and future career opportunities.

To empower Black children through AI education, it is crucial to create a supportive learning environment that fosters belonging and promotes their engagement. This can be achieved by incorporating culturally relevant content, diverse role models, and inclusive teaching practices into the curriculum. It is important to ensure that the materials used in AI education reflect the experiences and perspectives of Black children, allowing them to see themselves represented in the content.

Furthermore, fostering inclusivity requires addressing systemic barriers that hinder access to AI education for underrepresented communities. This includes providing resources such as scholarships, mentorship programs, and community partnerships that support Black children's participation in AI-related activities. Additionally, educators must receive training on cultural competency and inclusive pedagogies to effectively teach AI concepts in a manner that resonates with Black children.

Frequently Asked Questions

What Are the Potential Long-Term Effects of Teaching AI to Black Children at an Early Age?

The potential long-term effects of teaching AI to black children at an early age include opportunities for skill development, increased exposure to technology, potential career prospects, and the possibility of addressing racial disparities in the field of AI.

How Can AI Education Positively Impact the Representation of Black Individuals in the Field of Artificial Intelligence?

AI education can positively impact the representation of black individuals in the field of artificial intelligence by providing early exposure and opportunities for skills development, which can help bridge existing racial disparities and promote diversity within the industry.

Are There Any Specific Challenges or Barriers That Black Children May Face When Learning About AI?

Specific challenges or barriers that black children may face when learning about AI include limited access to resources, lack of representation in the field, racial bias in AI algorithms, and the need for culturally relevant and inclusive educational materials.

What Resources or Tools Are Available to Parents and Educators to Support AI Education for Black Children?

Resources and tools available to support AI education for black children include online platforms, coding programs, educational apps, and STEM-focused curricula. These resources aim to provide equal access and promote inclusivity in the field of AI education.

Can Early AI Education Contribute to Closing the Racial Achievement Gap in STEM Fields for Black Children?

Early AI education may contribute to closing the racial achievement gap in STEM fields for black children. This potential benefit arises from the exposure to advanced technology and computational thinking skills that can enhance their academic performance and future career opportunities.

Conclusion

In conclusion, teaching AI to black children at an early age is crucial for their empowerment and future success. By introducing AI concepts, we can break down misconceptions and equip them with valuable skills in this rapidly advancing field.

Through early AI education, black children can gain a competitive edge and contribute to the development of innovative solutions.

So, why wait? Let's ensure that every child, regardless of their background, has the opportunity to explore and excel in the world of AI.

The Growing Influence of AI in Various Aspects of Society

In today's rapidly evolving society, the influence of artificial intelligence (AI) continues to expand across various domains. Its impact can be observed in healthcare, education, business and industry, transportation, as well as social and environmental issues.

AI's growing presence has prompted researchers to explore its implications on society at large. This section aims to examine the multifaceted ways in which AI is shaping different aspects of our lives.

By delving into these areas, it becomes evident that AI's role is increasingly significant and cannot be ignored in the contemporary world.

Key Takeaways

- AI is playing a significant role in healthcare by improving diagnostic accuracy, enhancing patient monitoring, optimizing treatment plans, and analyzing vast amounts of data.
- In the field of education and learning, AI is providing personalized support to students, adapting instructional content based on individual needs, streamlining

the evaluation process, and creating inclusive environments for all students.

- AI is also making a significant impact in business and industry by automating routine tasks, analyzing large volumes of data, making data-driven decisions, and enhancing customer service through chatbots.
- In transportation, AI is optimizing routes and schedules, increasing safety through autonomous vehicles, promoting sustainable transportation solutions, and improving efficiency and travel times.

The Impact of AI in Healthcare

The impact of AI in healthcare is evident through its ability to improve diagnostic accuracy, enhance patient monitoring, and optimize treatment plans. Artificial intelligence has revolutionized the field of medicine by providing advanced technology that can analyze vast amounts of data and identify patterns that may not be easily discernible to human healthcare professionals. This enables AI systems to assist in the diagnosis of diseases with higher accuracy rates than traditional methods.

Furthermore, AI-powered monitoring systems allow for continuous tracking of patient health parameters, providing real-time updates to healthcare providers. By analyzing this data, AI algorithms can detect subtle changes in a patient's condition that may require immediate attention. This early detection can help prevent complications and improve overall patient outcomes.

In addition to diagnosis and monitoring, AI also plays a crucial role in optimizing treatment plans. Through machine learning algorithms, AI systems can analyze a patient's medical history, genetic information, and relevant research studies to develop personalized treatment options. These individualized approaches lead to more effective treatments with fewer side effects.

Overall, the impact of AI in healthcare is undeniable as it enhances diagnostic accuracy, improves patient monitoring practices, and optimizes treatment plans. Its integration into medical practice has the potential to transform healthcare delivery and improve outcomes for patients worldwide.

AI's Role in Education and Learning

One area where artificial intelligence has made significant advancements is in the field of education and learning. AI technologies are being increasingly integrated into educational institutions, transforming the way students learn and teachers instruct.

- AI-powered virtual assistants provide personalized support to students, offering immediate feedback on their performance and guiding them through the learning process.
- Intelligent tutoring systems utilize machine learning algorithms to adapt instructional content based on individual student needs, ensuring tailored and effective educational experiences.
- Automated grading systems streamline the evaluation process, freeing up valuable time for educators to focus on providing meaningful feedback and engaging with students.

These advancements in AI have the potential to revolutionize education by enhancing accessibility, personalization, and efficiency. Students can benefit from individualized instruction that caters to their unique strengths and weaknesses. Teachers can leverage AI tools to optimize their teaching strategies, saving time on administrative tasks while maximizing student engagement.

Moreover, these technologies foster a sense of belonging by creating inclusive environments where every student's needs are addressed. As AI continues to advance in education, it holds immense promise for creating a more equitable and effective learning experience for all individuals seeking knowledge.

AI in Business and Industry

AI's integration into business and industry has led to significant advancements, transforming the way organizations operate and making processes more efficient. The use of AI technology enables businesses to automate routine tasks, analyze large volumes of data, and make data-driven decisions. This has resulted in increased productivity, cost savings, and improved customer experiences.

One area where AI is making a significant impact is in customer service. Companies are using AI-powered chatbots to handle customer inquiries and provide personalized recommendations. These chatbots can quickly respond to customer queries, resolve issues efficiently, and deliver a seamless experience.

AI is also being used for predictive analytics in industries such as finance and marketing. By analyzing historical data patterns, AI algorithms can forecast market trends, identify potential risks or opportunities, and help businesses make informed decisions.

Furthermore, AI is revolutionizing the manufacturing sector through automation. Robots equipped with AI capabilities can perform repetitive tasks with precision and speed. This not only reduces human error but also increases production efficiency.

AI and Its Influence on Transportation

AI technology has revolutionized the transportation industry, enabling advancements in autonomous vehicles and intelligent traffic management systems. This technological innovation has had a profound impact on various aspects of transportation, providing numerous benefits and opportunities for improvement.

- **Efficiency**: AI-powered transportation systems optimize routes and schedules, reducing congestion and improving overall efficiency. Intelligent traffic management systems can analyze real-time data to dynamically adjust traffic signals, easing congestion and minimizing travel times.
- **Safety**: Autonomous vehicles equipped with AI algorithms have the potential to significantly reduce accidents caused by human error. These vehicles use sensors and advanced algorithms to detect obstacles, predict potential collisions, and make split-second decisions to avoid accidents.
- **Sustainability**: AI technology is also instrumental in promoting sustainable transportation solutions. Electric vehicle charging stations powered by AI algorithms can efficiently manage energy distribution, ensuring optimal utilization of renewable energy sources.

The integration of AI into the transportation industry not only enhances efficiency but also improves safety and promotes sustainability. As this technology continues to evolve, it holds great promise for transforming the way we commute and transport goods while creating a sense of belonging within a society that values progress and innovation.

AI's Contribution to Social and Environmental Issues

The incorporation of AI technology into transportation systems has had significant implications for addressing social and environmental issues. AI has the potential to contribute to a more sustainable and equitable society by improving efficiency, reducing emissions, and enhancing safety in transportation networks.

One area where AI can address social issues is through the optimization of traffic flow. By using real-time data and machine learning algorithms, AI can analyze traffic patterns and make predictions to optimize routes, reduce congestion, and minimize travel times. This not only improves the overall efficiency of transportation systems but also enhances accessibility for individuals with limited mobility or those who rely on public transportation.

Furthermore, AI can play a crucial role in reducing environmental impact by optimizing energy consumption in vehicles. Through advanced analytics and predictive modeling, AI can optimize fuel usage and suggest alternative modes of transport that are more environmentally friendly. Additionally, AI-powered systems can help monitor emissions from vehicles and enforce emission standards to ensure compliance with regulations.

Frequently Asked Questions

What Are the Potential Ethical Concerns Surrounding the Use of AI in Healthcare?

Potential ethical concerns surrounding the use of AI in healthcare include privacy and security risks, algorithm bias, lack of transparency, and the potential for AI to replace human judgment and decision-making.

How Can AI Be Used to Personalize Education and Cater to Individual Learning Needs?

The use of AI in education can lead to personalized learning experiences tailored to individual needs. By analyzing data and utilizing algorithms, AI systems can identify students' strengths and weaknesses, suggest customized learning materials, and provide real-time feedback for effective learning outcomes.

What Are Some Examples of How AI Is Being Implemented in Different Industries to Improve Efficiency and Productivity?

Examples of AI implementation in different industries to improve efficiency and productivity include automated customer service systems, predictive maintenance in manufacturing, algorithmic trading in finance, and machine learning algorithms for data analysis in healthcare.

How Is AI Technology Being Utilized to Enhance Transportation Systems and Address Traffic Congestion?

AI technology is being utilized to enhance transportation systems and address traffic congestion. Through advanced algorithms and machine learning, AI can optimize traffic flow, predict patterns, and suggest alternative routes, leading to improved efficiency and reduced congestion.

In What Ways Can AI Be Utilized to Address Social and Environmental Issues Such as Climate Change and Sustainability?

AI can be utilized to address social and environmental issues such as climate change and sustainability through various means. For instance, AI can assist in analyzing large amounts of data to identify patterns and trends, optimize resource allocation, and develop predictive models for better decision-making.

Conclusion

In conclusion, the growing influence of AI in various aspects of society is undeniable. From healthcare to education, business to transportation, and even social and environmental issues, AI has made significant contributions that have revolutionized these fields.

As we continue to witness the advancements and capabilities of AI, it leaves us wondering what the future holds for this technology. Will it continue to shape our world? Only time will tell.

But one thing is certain – the impact of AI is far-reaching, and its potential is limitless. Stay tuned as we uncover the mysteries that lie ahead.

The Underrepresentation of Black Individuals in AI and Technology Fields

In the realm of artificial intelligence (AI) and technology, there exists a disconcerting underrepresentation of black individuals.

This section aims to shed light on this historical context by examining the lack of diversity in these fields.

It will explore the challenges faced by black individuals in accessing AI and technology education, as well as analyze implicit bias and discrimination in hiring practices.

Furthermore, it will emphasize the importance of representation and discuss initiatives and programs addressing this underrepresentation.

Ultimately, this section seeks to envision steps towards creating a more inclusive AI and technology industry.

Key Takeaways

- Lack of diversity in AI and technology fields, predominantly occupied by individuals from privileged backgrounds.
- Limited opportunities for marginalized groups, including black individuals, in accessing education and professional opportunities.
- Implicit bias and discrimination in AI and technology hiring practices, leading to systemic barriers for black candidates.
- Importance of representation in AI and technology for fostering comprehensive understanding, mitigating bias, and driving progress and innovation

The Historical Context: Lack of Diversity in AI and Technology

The historical context reveals a marked lack of diversity in AI and technology fields, particularly with regards to the underrepresentation of black individuals. Throughout history, these fields have been predominantly occupied by individuals from privileged backgrounds, resulting in limited opportunities for marginalized groups, including black individuals. This lack of diversity has significant implications for the development and application of AI technologies.

One reason behind this underrepresentation is the systemic barriers that black individuals face in accessing education and professional opportunities. Limited access to quality education in STEM subjects creates a pipeline problem where fewer black students pursue careers in AI and technology. Additionally, unconscious biases within hiring processes reinforce existing disparities by favoring candidates from more traditional backgrounds.

Furthermore, historical exclusionary practices have created an environment that perpetuates inequality. Networks formed through personal connections play a critical role in career advancement, but exclusion from these networks further marginalizes black professionals. The absence of diverse voices leads to biased algorithms and technologies that fail to consider the needs and perspectives of all users.

Addressing this lack of diversity requires intentional efforts at multiple levels. Educational institutions must prioritize inclusivity by increasing access to quality STEM education for marginalized communities. Companies should implement fair hiring practices and actively seek out diverse talent pools. Moreover, fostering inclusive work environments can help create a sense of belonging where all employees feel valued regardless of their background.

Challenges Faced by Black Individuals in Accessing AI and Technology Education

A major obstacle that arises for minority groups, particularly those of African descent, when seeking to access education in AI and technology relates to the challenges they face. These challenges can impede their progress and contribute to the underrepresentation of black individuals in these fields.

1. Limited access to resources: Many black individuals lack access to quality educational resources, such as advanced STEM courses or specialized training programs in AI and technology. This limits their ability to acquire the necessary skills and knowledge.
2. Lack of representation: The scarcity of role models from similar backgrounds can make it difficult for aspiring black students to envision themselves succeeding in AI and technology fields. The absence of diverse mentors and leaders further reinforces feelings of exclusion.
3. Bias in recruitment processes: Discrimination during hiring or admission processes is another challenge faced by black individuals. Racial bias may lead to qualified candidates being overlooked or disregarded, perpetuating the underrepresentation issue.
4. Stereotypes and stigma: Negative stereotypes about intelligence or capabilities can create a hostile environment for black individuals pursuing education in AI and technology. This stigma discourages participation due to fear of failure or social isolation.

These challenges highlight the importance of addressing systemic barriers that hinder the inclusion of black individuals in AI and technology education and workforce opportunities. Creating an environment that values diversity, provides equal opportunities, and supports marginalized communities is crucial for fostering belongingness within these fields.

Implicit Bias and Discrimination in AI and Technology Hiring Practices

Implicit bias and discrimination in hiring practices within the AI and technology sector continues to perpetuate inequities and hinder diversity. Despite efforts to increase representation, black individuals are still significantly underrepresented in these fields. Research has shown that implicit biases, which are unconscious attitudes or stereotypes that affect our judgments and actions, often influence hiring decisions.

Studies have demonstrated that hiring managers may hold certain biases against black candidates due to societal stereotypes and preconceived notions about their abilities. These biases can lead to discriminatory practices such as overlooking qualified black applicants or subjecting them to more scrutiny during the selection process.

Moreover, research has shown that even when resumes are identical in terms of qualifications, black candidates are less likely to receive callbacks or job offers compared to white candidates. This suggests the presence of racial bias in hiring decisions within the AI and technology sector.

Addressing implicit bias and discrimination in hiring practices is crucial for promoting diversity and creating a sense of belonging for all individuals within these industries. Implementing strategies such as blind resume screening, diversity training for hiring managers, and establishing inclusive recruitment policies can help mitigate the effects of bias on candidate selection.

The Importance of Representation: Why Diversity Matters in AI and Technology

Representation and diversity play a crucial role in fostering innovation and driving progress in the AI and technology sectors. The underrepresentation of certain groups, such as black individuals, is a pressing issue that needs to be addressed. Here are four reasons why diversity matters in AI and technology:

1. Different Perspectives: A diverse workforce brings together individuals with unique experiences, backgrounds, and perspectives. This diversity of thought allows for a more comprehensive understanding of problems and facilitates creative solutions.
2. Avoiding Bias: AI systems can perpetuate biases if they are trained on data that lacks diverse representation. By including diverse voices in the development process, we can mitigate bias and ensure fairness in decision-making algorithms.
3. Meeting Global Needs: The users of AI technologies come from various cultural backgrounds and have different needs. Having a diverse team ensures that these technologies are inclusive, accessible, and cater to the needs of all users.
4. Enhanced Innovation: Studies have shown that diverse teams outperform homogeneous ones when it comes to innovation and problem-solving. Diverse perspectives foster creativity, drive collaboration, and lead to breakthrough ideas that benefit society as a whole.

Initiatives and Programs Addressing the Underrepresentation of Black Individuals in AI and Technology

To address the lack of diversity in the AI and technology sectors, various initiatives and programs have been implemented with the aim of increasing inclusion and representation. These efforts recognize the importance of creating a sense of belonging for underrepresented groups, particularly black individuals, within these fields.

One such initiative is the creation of mentorship programs that connect black students and professionals with experienced mentors who can provide guidance and support throughout their careers. These mentorship programs help to bridge the gap between academia and industry by offering valuable insights into career pathways, networking opportunities, and skill development.

Another approach involves establishing scholarship programs specifically targeted at black individuals pursuing studies in AI and technology-related disciplines. These scholarships not only provide financial assistance but also serve as a means to encourage more black students to pursue education in these fields. By removing financial barriers, these programs seek to increase access to education and create equal opportunities for all.

Furthermore, organizations are implementing outreach programs aimed at introducing AI and technology concepts to young black students from an early age. By exposing them to these subjects through workshops, summer camps, or coding clubs, these initiatives aim to spark interest and foster a sense of belonging among young black individuals.

Steps towards Creating a More Inclusive AI and Technology Industry

One approach towards creating a more inclusive AI and technology industry involves implementing diversity training programs for professionals in these fields. These programs aim to address the underrepresentation of marginalized groups, such as black individuals, by providing education and awareness about biases, stereotypes, and systemic barriers that may exist within the industry. The goal is to foster an environment where everyone feels valued, respected, and included.

To achieve this goal, several steps can be taken:

1. Raising Awareness: This involves educating professionals about the importance of diversity and inclusion in AI and technology industries. It aims to create a shared understanding of the benefits that diverse perspectives bring to innovation and problem-solving.
2. Unconscious Bias Training: By addressing unconscious biases that individuals may hold, this type of training helps professionals recognize their own biases and develop strategies to mitigate their impact on decision-making processes.
3. Promoting Inclusive Hiring Practices: Implementing policies that ensure a fair recruitment process can help increase representation of underrepresented groups in AI and technology fields. This includes actively seeking out diverse candidates, setting specific goals for diversity hiring, and examining potential biases in job descriptions.
4. Creating Supportive Networks: Encouraging the formation of networks or affinity groups within organizations can provide support, mentorship opportunities, and resources specifically tailored to the needs of underrepresented individuals.

Frequently Asked Questions

What Are Some Historical Examples of Underrepresentation of Black Individuals in AI and Technology Fields?

Historical examples of underrepresentation of Black individuals in AI and technology fields include limited access to education, discriminatory hiring practices, lack of mentorship opportunities, and biased algorithms that perpetuate systemic inequalities.

How Does the Lack of Diversity in AI and Technology Education Affect Black Individuals' Access to These Fields?

The lack of diversity in AI and technology education may hinder black individuals' access to these fields, impacting their representation. This issue requires attention to ensure equal opportunities and inclusivity for all aspiring professionals.

What Are Some Examples of Implicit Bias and Discrimination in AI and Technology Hiring Practices That Black Individuals Face?

Examples of implicit bias and discrimination in AI and technology hiring practices faced by black individuals include unequal access to education, biased algorithms perpetuating stereotypes, and lack of diverse representation in decision-making roles.

How Does Diversity in AI and Technology Contribute to Innovation and Problem-Solving?

Diversity in AI and technology fields contributes to innovation and problem-solving by bringing together individuals with different perspectives, experiences, and expertise. This heterogeneity enables the exploration of various solutions and fosters creativity, leading to more robust outcomes.

What Are Some Specific Initiatives and Programs That Are Currently Addressing the Underrepresentation of Black Individuals in AI and Technology Fields?

Several initiatives and programs are being implemented to address the underrepresentation of Black individuals in AI and technology fields. These efforts aim to increase diversity and inclusivity by providing opportunities, mentorship, and support for Black individuals pursuing careers in these areas.

Conclusion

In conclusion, the underrepresentation of black individuals in AI and technology fields is a result of historical lack of diversity, challenges in accessing education, implicit bias and discrimination in hiring practices.

The importance of representation cannot be overstated as it brings forth diverse perspectives, ideas, and innovation.

Initiatives and programs are being implemented to address this issue and steps are being taken towards creating a more inclusive industry.

As the saying goes, 'Diversity is the key to unlocking our collective potential.'

The Benefits and Social Implications of Teaching Black Children AI Skills

In recent years, the field of artificial intelligence (AI) has gained significant attention for its potential to transform various aspects of society. One area of focus is the education sector, where AI skills are increasingly being recognized as essential for future success.

This section aims to examine the benefits and social implications of teaching black children AI skills. By exploring the importance of equitable AI education, empowering black children through these skills, closing the racial gap in tech, enhancing career opportunities, addressing bias and ethical considerations, and fostering innovation and creativity, this section seeks to shed light on the potential impact that AI education can have on black children's lives.

Key Takeaways

- Equitable AI education ensures equal opportunities for black children.
- Acquiring AI competencies instills a sense of belonging and empowerment.
- AI education initiatives increase representation of underrepresented communities.
- Proficiency in AI opens numerous career pathways.

The Importance of Equitable AI Education

Equitable AI education is crucial for ensuring equal opportunities and empowering black children to actively participate in the development and utilization of artificial intelligence technologies. By providing a comprehensive and inclusive education in AI, we can address the existing disparities and promote diversity within this rapidly evolving field.

AI technology has become increasingly prevalent in various sectors, ranging from healthcare to finance, influencing decision-making processes that shape our society. However, without equitable access to AI education, black children may be left behind, exacerbating existing inequalities. Thus, it is imperative that we prioritize their inclusion by offering educational programs tailored to their specific needs.

Through equitable AI education, black children can develop critical skills necessary for future employment opportunities. By understanding how AI systems work and being able to contribute to their design and implementation, they can actively shape the development of these technologies rather than passively consuming them. This empowers them as active participants in technological advancements rather than mere bystanders.

Moreover, equitable AI education fosters a sense of belonging by acknowledging the unique experiences and perspectives of black students. It creates an environment where they feel valued and included in discussions surrounding AI ethics, biases, and social implications. This sense of belonging encourages greater engagement with the subject matter and promotes confidence in their abilities to navigate this complex field.

Empowering Black Children through AI Skills

Promoting the acquisition of artificial intelligence (AI) competencies among Black youth can provide them with empowering opportunities for personal growth and professional development. AI skills are increasingly in demand across various industries, and by equipping Black children with these competencies, they can become active participants in shaping the future of technology. By engaging in AI education, Black youth can gain valuable knowledge and skills that enable them to navigate and contribute to a rapidly evolving digital landscape.

Acquiring AI competencies not only offers practical benefits but also instills a sense of belonging and empowerment. By being knowledgeable in AI, Black children can find their place within technological communities and foster connections with like-minded individuals who share their interests. This sense of belonging is crucial as it promotes self-confidence, resilience, and motivation to pursue further learning opportunities. Additionally, acquiring AI skills helps counteract historical barriers that have limited representation of Black individuals within the tech industry.

Moreover, empowering Black children through AI skills creates pathways for personal growth and professional development. As technology continues to shape our world, proficiency in AI opens doors to diverse career prospects ranging from data analysis to algorithm design. Equipped with these skills, Black youth can actively contribute to innovation while simultaneously challenging existing biases embedded within technologies.

Closing the Racial Gap in Tech with AI Education

Closing the racial gap in the tech industry can be achieved through comprehensive AI education initiatives that aim to address historical disparities and increase representation of underrepresented communities. These initiatives have the potential to bring about numerous benefits and positive social implications:

- Increased diversity: By providing AI education opportunities to underrepresented communities, there will be a greater representation of diverse perspectives in the tech industry. This can lead to more inclusive technological development and decision-making processes.
- Economic empowerment: Access to AI skills can create new opportunities for individuals from marginalized backgrounds, allowing them to secure higher-paying jobs and achieve economic mobility.
- Closing the knowledge gap: Historically, marginalized communities have faced limited access to quality education in STEM fields. AI education programs specifically targeted towards these communities can help bridge this knowledge gap by equipping individuals with relevant skills.
- Reducing bias in algorithms: Greater representation of underrepresented groups in AI development can help mitigate biases that are often embedded within algorithms. This is crucial for ensuring fair and equitable outcomes across various domains, such as hiring practices or criminal justice systems.
- Fostering innovation: Diverse perspectives foster creativity and innovation. By increasing representation through AI education initiatives, we create an environment that encourages novel ideas and solutions for complex technological challenges.

Enhancing Career Opportunities for Black Children through AI Skills

Enhancing career opportunities for Black individuals can be achieved through the acquisition of AI skills, providing them with the necessary knowledge and expertise to thrive in the tech industry. In recent years, there has been a growing recognition of the underrepresentation of Black individuals in technology-related careers. This lack of representation not only perpetuates systemic inequalities but also hinders diverse perspectives and innovation within the industry.

By teaching Black children AI skills, we can bridge this racial gap and create a more inclusive and equitable tech workforce. With AI becoming increasingly prevalent across various industries, having proficiency in this field opens up numerous career pathways. As technology continues to advance, professionals with AI skills are in high demand, making it a valuable asset for job seekers.

Moreover, acquiring AI skills empowers Black individuals to navigate an industry that has historically excluded them. By equipping them with these capabilities, they gain confidence in their technical abilities and become better positioned to overcome barriers they may face due to systemic racism.

Overall, teaching Black children AI skills not only enhances their career prospects but also contributes to building a more diverse and inclusive tech sector. It provides opportunities for belonging by addressing the historical disadvantages faced by this community and creating avenues for success in an ever-evolving digital world.

Addressing Bias and Ethical Considerations in AI Education

Addressing bias and ethical considerations in AI education requires a comprehensive approach that includes curriculum development, teacher training, and ongoing assessment of instructional materials. It is crucial to ensure that AI education is delivered in a fair and unbiased manner, promoting inclusivity and fostering a sense of belonging for all students.

To achieve this, the following strategies should be implemented:

- Incorporate diverse perspectives: Integrate multiple viewpoints into the curriculum to reflect the experiences and contributions of different groups, including those historically underrepresented in the field.
- Teach critical thinking skills: Enable students to analyze AI technologies critically, understand their limitations, and identify potential biases or ethical concerns.
- Foster open discussions: Create an inclusive classroom environment where students feel comfortable expressing their opinions and engaging in dialogue about bias and ethics in AI.
- Provide professional development for teachers: Offer training programs that enhance teachers' understanding of bias and ethical considerations in AI education, enabling them to effectively address these topics with their students.
- Continuously evaluate instructional materials: Regularly review textbooks, online resources, and other teaching materials for bias or outdated information to ensure they align with current standards of fairness and inclusivity.

Fostering Innovation and Creativity in Black Children through AI Skills

To cultivate innovation and creativity in individuals from Black communities, it is imperative to provide them with opportunities to develop their proficiency in the application of artificial intelligence. By equipping Black children with AI skills, we can empower them to become active participants in the rapidly evolving technological landscape. Access to AI education not only enhances their ability to navigate and thrive in a digital society but also enables them to contribute innovative solutions that address societal challenges.

Incorporating AI education into the curriculum can foster critical thinking, problem-solving, and computational skills among Black children. It encourages them to explore new possibilities, experiment with data analysis techniques, and develop algorithms that can augment human capabilities. This exposure nurtures creativity by challenging traditional approaches and fostering an entrepreneurial mindset.

Furthermore, providing Black children with AI skills creates a sense of belonging within the larger tech community. It allows them to engage with peers who share similar interests and aspirations, building networks for collaboration and support. Representation within the field also promotes diversity of thought and perspectives, leading to more inclusive AI applications that consider multiple viewpoints.

Frequently Asked Questions

How Can AI Education Benefit Children from Other Racial Backgrounds?

The benefits of AI education extend beyond racial boundaries, fostering a sense of inclusivity and promoting diversity in the field. By equipping children from various racial backgrounds with AI skills, they gain access to new opportunities and contribute to the advancement of society.

What Are Some Potential Challenges or Barriers in Implementing AI Education for Black Children?

Potential challenges or barriers in implementing AI education for black children may include limited access to resources, lack of representation in the field, existing educational disparities, cultural biases, and inequitable distribution of opportunities, which could perpetuate racial inequalities.

Are There Any Specific AI Tools or Platforms That Are Recommended for Teaching Black Children AI Skills?

Specific AI tools and platforms recommended for teaching AI skills to black children have not been discussed in the given context. Further research is needed to identify such tools and platforms that may be beneficial in this regard.

How Can AI Education Help in Addressing Systemic Racism and Inequality in the Education System?

AI education has the potential to address systemic racism and inequality in the education system by providing access to technological tools and skills that can empower black children. This can lead to increased opportunities, improved academic performance, and a more equitable learning environment.

Is There Any Ongoing Research or Initiatives Focused on Improving AI Education Specifically for Black Children?

Ongoing research and initiatives are focused on improving AI education specifically for black children. These efforts aim to address systemic racism and inequality in the education system, offering opportunities for skill development and combating disparities in access.

Conclusion

In conclusion, the benefits and social implications of teaching AI skills to black children are vast. By providing equitable AI education, we can empower these young individuals and close the racial gap in the tech industry.

Moreover, AI skills enhance career opportunities for black children and foster innovation and creativity. However, it is crucial to address bias and ethical considerations in AI education to ensure a fair and just society.

Let us embrace this opportunity to shape a future where all children can thrive through AI knowledge.

CHAPTER 1: THE POWER
OF EARLY EDUCATION

The Importance of Early Education in Shaping a Child's Cognitive Abilities

In the realm of child development, the significance of early education in shaping a child's cognitive abilities cannot be overlooked. Numerous studies have demonstrated that during the critical period of cognitive development, which occurs in the early years of life, children are highly receptive to learning and experience rapid brain growth.

This section aims to explore the impact of early education on brain development, focusing on how it builds strong foundations for cognitive skills such as memory, attention, problem-solving, language, and communication abilities. By examining empirical evidence and theoretical frameworks, this discussion will shed light on why early education holds paramount importance in fostering optimal cognitive development in children.

Key Takeaways

- Early childhood is a critical period for cognitive development, and early education plays a crucial role in shaping a child's cognitive abilities.
- Enriched environments and positive relationships with caregivers in early education promote optimal brain development and foster the development of executive functioning skills.
- Early education programs focus on developing memory and attention skills through strategies such as repetition, visual aids, and cooperative play.
- Problem-solving skills are essential in early education, and activities involving critical thinking, logical reasoning, and collaboration enhance problem-solving abilities.

The Critical Period for Cognitive Development

The critical period for cognitive development refers to a specific time frame in early childhood during which the brain is particularly receptive to acquiring and developing various cognitive abilities. This period is characterized by rapid growth and significant changes in neural connections, allowing for the formation of complex cognitive processes. It is widely accepted among researchers that early experiences and environmental influences play a crucial role in shaping a child's cognitive abilities.

During this critical period, children have an increased capacity for learning and absorbing information from their surroundings. The brain undergoes important structural changes, such as synaptic pruning and myelination, which enhance neural efficiency and facilitate more efficient information processing. This heightened plasticity allows for the acquisition of language skills, problem-solving abilities, memory formation, attention control, and other fundamental cognitive functions.

Research has shown that the quality of early education programs can significantly impact a child's cognitive development. Enriched environments that provide stimulating activities, opportunities for exploration, social interaction, and exposure to language-rich settings promote optimal brain development during this critical period. Additionally, positive relationships with caregivers or teachers can foster emotional well-being and create an environment conducive to learning.

The Impact of Early Education on Brain Development

One key factor to consider when examining the impact of early education on brain development is its potential to significantly influence the cognitive capabilities of individuals. Early education programs provide a structured and stimulating environment that promotes cognitive growth through various activities and interactions.

Enhanced neural connections: Engaging in educational activities during early years can lead to the establishment of stronger neural connections in the brain, particularly in areas responsible for language, problem-solving, and memory. These strengthened connections lay a solid foundation for future learning and intellectual development.

Improved executive functioning: Early education fosters the development of executive functions such as attention, self-control, and working memory. These skills are crucial for academic success and overall well-being throughout life.

Social-emotional skills: Early education also plays a vital role in nurturing social-emotional skills like empathy, cooperation, and self-regulation. These skills contribute to positive relationships with peers and adults, making children feel a sense of belonging within their communities.

Building Strong Foundations: Early Learning and Cognitive Skills

Building strong foundations for cognitive development in early childhood involves providing a structured and stimulating learning environment that promotes the growth of neural connections, executive functioning skills, and social-emotional capabilities. This approach recognizes the significance of early education in shaping a child's cognitive abilities.

A structured learning environment provides children with consistent routines and clear expectations, allowing them to develop self-regulation skills. It helps children feel secure and supported, which is crucial for optimal brain development. Furthermore, a stimulating learning environment offers various opportunities for exploration and discovery. This exposure enhances synaptic connections in the brain, leading to increased cognitive capacities.

Executive functioning skills play a vital role in cognitive development as they enable individuals to plan, organize, problem-solve, and exhibit self-control. Early education programs that focus on developing these skills contribute to better academic achievement later in life.

In addition to cognitive abilities, early education also emphasizes social-emotional capabilities. Children learn how to interact with peers and adults through positive relationships built within the learning environment. These interactions foster empathy, cooperation, communication skills, and emotional regulation – all essential components of healthy social-emotional development.

The Role of Early Education in Enhancing Memory and Attention

Enhancing memory and attention in early childhood is a key focus of educational interventions aimed at promoting optimal cognitive development. The role of early education in shaping these cognitive abilities cannot be overstated. It is during the early years that children's brains are rapidly developing, and the experiences they have during this critical period can have long-lasting effects on their cognitive functioning.

1. Early education provides a structured and stimulating environment that promotes memory and attention skills. Children engage in activities that require them to pay attention, follow instructions, and remember information, which helps strengthen these cognitive processes.
2. Interactions with teachers and peers in early education settings foster social connections that enhance memory and attention abilities. Through cooperative play, group discussions, and collaborative problem-solving tasks, children learn how to focus their attention on relevant information while ignoring distractions.
3. Early education programs often incorporate strategies such as repetition, mnemonic devices, and visual aids to support memory encoding and retrieval processes. These techniques help children remember important concepts or information by providing them with effective tools for organizing and retaining knowledge.

Early Education and the Development of Problem-Solving Skills

The development of problem-solving skills is an essential aspect of early education. It equips young children with the ability to analyze and solve complex tasks or challenges. Problem-solving involves applying cognitive processes to identify obstacles, generate potential solutions, evaluate their effectiveness, and select the most appropriate one.

Early education programs play a vital role in fostering these skills through various activities and experiences that encourage critical thinking and logical reasoning.

One way that early education promotes problem-solving abilities is by creating an environment that encourages exploration, curiosity, and experimentation. Such an atmosphere stimulates children's natural inclination to question and explore their surroundings. Additionally, educators can design activities that involve puzzles, games, or open-ended tasks which require children to think critically and find creative solutions.

Furthermore, collaborative learning experiences in early education settings provide opportunities for children to engage in problem-solving together. Collaboration enhances problem-solving skills by fostering communication, teamwork, negotiation, and compromise among peers. Through group work or projects that necessitate brainstorming ideas or solving problems collectively, children learn how to listen actively to others' perspectives while contributing their own insights.

How Early Education Shapes Language and Communication Abilities

Early education plays a crucial role in shaping a child's cognitive abilities, including their language and communication skills. Language development begins at an early age and is strongly influenced by the environment in which a child grows up.

Enriched vocabulary: Early education provides children with exposure to a wide range of vocabulary words, helping them develop a richer and more diverse lexicon. This expanded vocabulary enhances their ability to express themselves effectively and understand others.

Effective communication skills: Through interactions with teachers and peers, children learn how to convey their thoughts, ideas, and feelings in a clear and coherent manner. They also acquire important social skills such as turn-taking during conversations, active listening, and non-verbal communication cues.

Cultural belonging: Early education can foster a sense of belonging by introducing children to different cultural perspectives through stories, songs, and activities. This exposure helps them develop respect for diversity while building connections with others who may come from different backgrounds.

Frequently Asked Questions

What Are Some Strategies Parents Can Use to Support Their Child's Cognitive Development at Home?

Strategies to support a child's cognitive development at home include engaging in activities that promote critical thinking, problem-solving, and memory skills. Providing opportunities for play, reading, and exploring the environment can also contribute to their overall cognitive growth.

Are There Any Long-Term Benefits of Early Education on Cognitive Abilities?

There are long-term benefits of early education on cognitive abilities. Research has shown that children who receive quality early education experience improvements in their cognitive functioning, such as language development and problem-solving skills, which can have lasting effects into adulthood.

How Does Early Education Specifically Impact the Development of Creativity and Imagination?

Early education has a significant impact on the development of creativity and imagination. Studies have shown that children who receive early education are more likely to demonstrate higher levels of creative thinking and imaginative play compared to those who do not have access to such educational opportunities.

Can Early Education Help Prevent or Address Learning Disabilities and Cognitive Delays?

Early education can play a crucial role in addressing and preventing learning disabilities and cognitive delays. By providing early intervention and targeted support, educators can identify and address developmental issues, allowing children to reach their full cognitive potential.

Is There a Recommended Age for Children to Start Receiving Early Education for Optimal Cognitive Development?

There is no universally recommended age for optimal cognitive development through early education. However, research suggests that the earlier children start receiving quality early education, the greater potential for positive impact on their cognitive abilities.

Conclusion

Early education plays a crucial role in shaping a child's cognitive abilities. During the critical period of cognitive development, early education provides essential stimulation for brain development. It helps build strong foundations for cognitive skills such as memory, attention, problem-solving, and language abilities.

An interesting statistic to highlight is that children who receive high-quality early education are more likely to graduate from high school and have higher academic achievement throughout their lives compared to those who do not receive such opportunities. This highlights the importance of investing in early education for long-term success.

The Concept of "Critical Periods" in Brain Development and Skill Acquisition

The concept of 'critical periods' in brain development and skill acquisition holds great significance in understanding the complex processes underlying human cognitive growth.

These critical periods, characterized by heightened neural plasticity and sensitivity to environmental stimuli, play a crucial role in shaping the trajectory of brain development and facilitating the acquisition of various skills.

By exploring the factors that influence critical periods and identifying their specific timings for different skills, researchers can gain valuable insights into optimizing brain development and enhancing skill acquisition during these sensitive phases.

Key Takeaways

- Critical periods determine the optimal time for acquiring skills and abilities.
- During critical periods, the brain is highly receptive to environmental stimuli.
- Permanent connections are formed during critical periods, shaping cognitive abilities.
- Exposure to rich linguistic environments or early musical training affects skill acquisition timing.

The Significance of Critical Periods in Brain Development

The significance of critical periods in brain development lies in their role in determining the optimal time for acquiring certain skills and abilities. Critical periods are specific time windows during which the brain is particularly sensitive to environmental stimuli, allowing for efficient learning and skill acquisition. During these critical periods, neural circuits undergo rapid growth and refinement, resulting in the formation of permanent connections that shape an individual's cognitive abilities.

One example of a critical period is language acquisition. Research has shown that there is a specific window of time during early childhood when children are highly receptive to language input from their environment. This critical period allows children to acquire language effortlessly and with great proficiency. If this window is missed or not adequately stimulated, individuals may struggle with language acquisition later in life.

Another important critical period occurs during early visual development. In this stage, the visual cortex undergoes significant changes based on visual experiences. Deprivation of visual input during this critical period can lead to irreversible deficits in vision.

Understanding the significance of these critical periods in brain development is crucial for educators, parents, and policymakers as it emphasizes the importance of providing appropriate stimulation and opportunities for skill acquisition at the right developmental stages. By capitalizing on these sensitive periods, individuals can maximize their potential for learning and cognitive growth.

Understanding the Role of Critical Periods in Skill Acquisition

Understanding the role of critical periods in skill acquisition involves investigating the time-sensitive windows during which individuals are most receptive to acquiring specific skills. Critical periods refer to specific developmental stages when the brain is particularly sensitive to learning and adapting to new experiences. During these periods, the neural circuits responsible for acquiring a particular skill are more easily molded and modified by environmental influences.

Research suggests that critical periods play a crucial role in various domains of skill acquisition, such as language development, music training, and visual perception. For example, children exposed to a rich linguistic environment during the first few years of life have a greater likelihood of developing strong language skills compared to those who miss this critical period. Similarly, individuals who receive musical training during early childhood show enhanced musical abilities later in life.

It is important to note that while critical periods provide a unique opportunity for skill acquisition, they also imply limitations. Once these sensitive windows close, it becomes increasingly difficult for individuals to acquire certain skills or reach the same level of proficiency as those who experienced them during their respective critical periods.

Overall, understanding the role of critical periods in skill acquisition sheds light on both the potential and constraints associated with different stages of human development. Recognizing these time-sensitive windows can inform targeted interventions and educational strategies aimed at optimizing skill acquisition processes throughout an individual's lifespan.

Factors Influencing Critical Periods in Brain Development

Factors influencing the timing and duration of sensitive windows in human brain development have been the focus of extensive research. These critical periods, characterized by heightened neuroplasticity and susceptibility to environmental influences, play a crucial role in shaping neural circuits underlying various cognitive functions.

Several factors are known to influence the establishment and closure of these critical periods.

One key factor is genetic predisposition. Studies have shown that certain genes are involved in regulating the timing and duration of critical periods. For example, mutations in genes such as FoxP2 have been linked to alterations in language acquisition during early childhood. Additionally, epigenetic modifications can also modulate the expression of critical period-related genes.

Environmental factors also play a significant role. Sensory input and experiences during specific developmental stages can shape synaptic connectivity and refine neural circuits. For instance, visual deprivation during infancy can lead to permanent deficits in visual acuity due to disrupted ocular dominance plasticity.

Furthermore, social interaction and cultural context can impact the timing and duration of sensitive windows in brain development. Peer relationships, parental care, socio-economic status, and cultural practices all contribute to shaping sensory experiences that influence critical period plasticity.

Understanding these factors is crucial for developing interventions aimed at optimizing brain development during sensitive periods. By identifying genetic markers and designing enriched environments tailored to individual needs, we may enhance neurodevelopmental outcomes for individuals who desire belonging within their communities.

Identifying Critical Periods for Specific Skills

Identifying the optimal time windows for skill acquisition is a key area of research in studying the developmental trajectories of specific abilities. Understanding when specific skills are most easily acquired can have important implications for educational interventions and the design of instructional programs. Researchers have used various methods to identify critical periods for different skills, such as language acquisition, musical ability, and visual perception.

For example, studies on language acquisition suggest that children have a sensitive period during which they are particularly adept at acquiring new languages. This period typically occurs between infancy and early adolescence, with language learning becoming more challenging after puberty. Similarly, research on musical ability has shown that there may be a critical period during childhood when individuals are more receptive to developing musical talents.

In addition to age-related factors, other variables such as environmental influences and individual differences can also impact the identification of critical periods for skill acquisition. For instance, exposure to rich linguistic environments or early musical training may affect the timing and ease with which certain skills can be acquired.

Overall, identifying critical periods for specific skills involves examining multiple factors including age-related changes, environmental influences, and individual differences. These findings contribute to our understanding of how skill development unfolds over time and inform strategies for optimizing learning opportunities during these sensitive periods.

Harnessing Critical Periods for Optimal Brain Development and Skill Acquisition

Leveraging the sensitive windows of development can have significant implications for optimizing learning outcomes and enhancing cognitive abilities. Understanding and harnessing critical periods in brain development and skill acquisition allows individuals to capitalize on periods of heightened neuroplasticity, thus maximizing their potential for learning and acquiring new skills. During these critical periods, the brain exhibits a heightened capacity for synaptic connections, neural circuit formation, and restructuring, enabling efficient skill acquisition.

Research suggests that early childhood is a particularly crucial period for brain development and the acquisition of fundamental skills such as language acquisition. For example, studies have shown that exposure to language during infancy is essential for developing strong language skills later in life. Similarly, early musical training has been found to enhance auditory processing abilities due to the plasticity of the auditory cortex during this developmental stage.

By identifying critical periods specific to different skills, educators and caregivers can design targeted interventions and provide appropriate stimuli during these sensitive windows. For instance, implementing immersive language programs or music education during early childhood may optimize language proficiency or musical aptitude respectively.

Moreover, understanding critical periods can also inform intervention strategies for individuals with neurodevelopmental disorders. Providing targeted interventions during sensitive periods may promote more effective remediation or compensation strategies for individuals with conditions such as dyslexia or autism spectrum disorder.

Frequently Asked Questions

What Are the Long-Term Effects of Missing Critical Periods in Brain Development?

The long-term effects of missing critical periods in brain development are not yet fully understood. However, research suggests that it can lead to difficulties in acquiring certain skills and may have lasting impacts on cognitive and behavioral functions.

How Do Critical Periods in Brain Development Differ from Sensitive Periods?

Critical periods in brain development differ from sensitive periods in that they are specific time windows during which certain experiences or stimuli have an especially strong impact on the development of particular skills or functions.

Are Critical Periods the Same for Every Individual, or Do They Vary?

Critical periods in brain development and skill acquisition may vary among individuals. While certain critical periods are biologically determined, individual differences in genetics, environmental factors, and experiences can influence the timing and duration of these sensitive periods.

Can Critical Periods Be Extended or Altered Through Interventions or Therapies?

Critical periods in brain development and skill acquisition refer to specific time frames during which the brain is most sensitive to acquiring certain skills. It is debated whether interventions or therapies can extend or alter these critical periods.

Are There Any Critical Periods for Emotional or Social Development, or Are They Primarily Related to Cognitive Skills?

Critical periods in brain development and skill acquisition are primarily related to cognitive skills, but there is evidence suggesting critical periods for emotional and social development as well. For example, studies have shown that early neglect can lead to long-term emotional deficits.

Conclusion

In conclusion, the concept of 'critical periods' in brain development and skill acquisition plays a vital role in shaping an individual's cognitive abilities. These specific time windows allow for optimal learning and development, but they are also influenced by various factors such as genetics and environmental stimuli.

While some may argue that critical periods limit the potential for learning later in life, it is important to recognize that these sensitive periods provide unique opportunities for acquiring complex skills. By understanding and harnessing critical periods, we can enhance brain development and maximize our potential for skill acquisition throughout life.

Successful Examples of Early Education Programs for Black Children from Disadvantaged Backgrounds

Early education plays a crucial role in the development and success of black children from disadvantaged backgrounds. This section aims to showcase successful examples of early education programs specifically designed for this demographic.

By examining accessible programs, effective strategies, culturally responsive approaches, collaborative engagement with parents and caregivers, as well as evaluation measures, we can gain insight into how these programs empower black children to overcome barriers and achieve academic excellence.

Through highlighting these achievements, this section contributes to the broader conversation on reducing educational disparities among marginalized communities.

Key Takeaways

- High-quality early education experiences have a significant impact on the academic and socio-emotional development of black children from disadvantaged backgrounds.
- Accessible early education programs such as Head Start, and the Harlem Children's Zone Project address multiple barriers faced by black children and provide comprehensive services.
- Culturally responsive curriculum and instruction, inclusive learning environments, and reduced racial disparities in disciplinary actions are effective strategies in early education programs for black children from disadvantaged backgrounds.
- Collaborative approaches that engage parents and caregivers, build strong partnerships between home and school, and empower parents to contribute their knowledge and expertise are crucial in supporting the educational development of black children from disadvantaged backgrounds.

Recognizing the Importance of Early Education for Black Children from Disadvantaged Backgrounds

Recognizing the importance of early education for black children from disadvantaged backgrounds entails acknowledging the significant impact it can have on their academic and socio-emotional development. Research has consistently shown that children who receive high-quality early education experiences are more likely to succeed academically and develop strong social skills. For black children from disadvantaged backgrounds, access to quality early education programs is crucial in addressing the achievement gap and promoting equitable opportunities.

Early education provides a foundation for lifelong learning by fostering cognitive, language, and socio-emotional development during the critical early years. It offers an environment where children can develop essential skills such as problem-solving, critical thinking, and self-regulation. Additionally, quality early education programs emphasize cultural sensitivity and inclusivity, creating an environment where all children feel valued and supported.

Moreover, early education programs play a pivotal role in mitigating the impact of adverse childhood experiences (ACEs) that disproportionately affect black children from disadvantaged backgrounds. By providing a nurturing and stimulating environment with trained educators who understand trauma-informed care, these programs can help mitigate the negative effects of ACEs on academic performance and socio-emotional well-being.

Overcoming Barriers: Accessible Early Education Programs for Black Children from Disadvantaged Backgrounds

Addressing the challenges faced by black children from disadvantaged backgrounds, accessible early education initiatives have been implemented to promote equitable access to educational opportunities. These programs aim to provide a strong foundation for learning and development, recognizing the importance of early education in shaping a child's future success.

One successful example is the Head Start program, which was established in 1965 as part of President Lyndon B. Johnson's War on Poverty. Designed specifically for children from low-income families, Head Start offers comprehensive services that address not only educational needs but also health, nutrition, and social-emotional development. By providing high-quality early education experiences, Head Start aims to narrow the achievement gap and improve long-term outcomes for these children.

Another noteworthy initiative is the Harlem Children's Zone (HCZ) Project. HCZ takes a holistic approach by offering a range of educational and social services to children and families living in Harlem. By providing access to high-quality pre-kindergarten programs, parenting workshops, health services, and community support networks, HCZ seeks to break the cycle of poverty and empower individuals to reach their full potential.

These accessible early education programs recognize that black children from disadvantaged backgrounds often face multiple barriers that limit their access to quality education. By addressing these challenges head-on through targeted interventions and comprehensive support systems, these initiatives strive towards creating an inclusive educational environment where all children can thrive academically and socially.

Empowering Success: Effective Strategies in Early Education Programs for Black Children from Disadvantaged Backgrounds

Empowering success in early education for black children from disadvantaged backgrounds requires the implementation of effective strategies that promote equitable access to educational opportunities and address the unique challenges faced by these students.

One such strategy is the provision of high-quality, culturally responsive curriculum and instruction. This includes incorporating diverse literature, history, and cultural experiences into classroom activities to foster a sense of belonging and relevance for black children.

Additionally, establishing strong partnerships between schools, families, and communities can support the holistic development of black children by providing resources, guidance, and support networks.

Another crucial element is ensuring that teachers are equipped with the knowledge and skills necessary to effectively teach black children from disadvantaged backgrounds. Professional development programs can provide educators with culturally relevant teaching practices that recognize and value the strengths of these students.

Furthermore, creating inclusive learning environments that celebrate diversity and promote positive racial identity development can enhance engagement and motivation among black children.

Finally, it is essential to address systemic barriers that disproportionately affect black children from disadvantaged backgrounds. This includes advocating for equitable funding distribution across schools and districts to ensure adequate resources are available to support their educational needs. Policymakers must also consider policies that reduce racial disparities in disciplinary actions within educational settings.

Promoting Cultural Competence: Culturally Responsive Early Education Programs for Black Children from Disadvantaged Backgrounds

Promoting cultural competence in early education involves the incorporation of culturally responsive practices and strategies to meet the unique needs of black children from disadvantaged backgrounds. By embracing cultural diversity and understanding the various experiences that shape these children's lives, educators can create inclusive learning environments that foster a sense of belonging and support their overall development.

Here are three key elements of culturally responsive early education programs for black children from disadvantaged backgrounds:

- Culturally relevant curriculum: Incorporating materials, activities, and resources that reflect the language, traditions, histories, and experiences of black cultures can enhance engagement and facilitate meaningful connections between students' identities and their learning.
- Multicultural perspectives: Encouraging diverse viewpoints and promoting an appreciation for different cultures helps cultivate empathy, respect, and understanding among students. This can be achieved through discussions, guest speakers or performers from different cultural backgrounds.
- Community involvement: Engaging families and local community members in the educational process helps build strong partnerships between home and school. Involving parents as active participants empowers them to contribute their knowledge and expertise while also reinforcing cultural values within the educational setting.

Engaging Parents and Caregivers: Collaborative Approaches in Early Education Programs for Black Children from Disadvantaged Backgrounds

Engaging parents and caregivers in collaborative approaches within early education settings fosters a sense of shared responsibility for the educational development of black children from disadvantaged backgrounds. Research has shown that when parents and caregivers are actively involved in their child's education, it leads to improved academic outcomes and overall well-being.

Collaborative approaches involve creating partnerships between educators, parents, and caregivers to establish open lines of communication, share information about the child's progress, and jointly develop strategies to support their learning.

In these collaborative approaches, educators should create a welcoming and inclusive environment that values the perspectives and experiences of all families. They should actively seek input from parents and caregivers regarding their goals, concerns, and aspirations for their child's education. This can be done through regular meetings, workshops, or even home visits. By involving parents and caregivers in decision-making processes related to curriculum planning or program evaluation, they feel a sense of ownership over their child's education.

Furthermore, providing opportunities for parents and caregivers to connect with each other can foster a sense of belonging within the early education community. This can be achieved through parent support groups or family events where they can share experiences, resources, and build social networks.

Ultimately, by engaging parents and caregivers in collaborative approaches within early education programs for black children from disadvantaged backgrounds promotes a sense of belonging and shared responsibility towards their educational development.

Measuring Impact: Evaluating the Success of Early Education Programs for Black Children from Disadvantaged Backgrounds

The previous subtopic discussed the importance of engaging parents and caregivers in early education programs for black children from disadvantaged backgrounds. This collaborative approach is essential for creating a supportive learning environment.

In this section, we will explore the next step in evaluating the success of these programs: measuring their impact.

Measuring the impact of early education programs is crucial to determine their effectiveness and make informed decisions regarding program improvements. It allows educators, policymakers, and stakeholders to assess whether these initiatives are achieving their intended outcomes and benefiting black children from disadvantaged backgrounds.

To evaluate the success of early education programs for black children from disadvantaged backgrounds, several key measures can be considered:

- Academic achievement: Assessing students' progress in core subjects such as reading, writing, math, and science.
- Social-emotional development: Evaluating students' ability to manage emotions, form positive relationships with peers and teachers, and exhibit appropriate behavior.
- Long-term outcomes: Tracking students' educational attainment, career prospects, and overall well-being beyond early childhood.

Frequently Asked Questions

What Are Some Common Challenges Faced by Black Children from Disadvantaged Backgrounds When Accessing Early Education Programs?

Black children from disadvantaged backgrounds commonly face challenges when accessing early education programs, including limited access to quality programs, lack of financial resources for enrollment, systemic inequalities in education, and cultural biases that may hinder their educational opportunities.

How Can Early Education Programs Effectively Address the Cultural Needs and Backgrounds of Black Children from Disadvantaged Backgrounds?

Effective early education programs can address the cultural needs and backgrounds of black children from disadvantaged backgrounds by incorporating culturally responsive teaching practices, engaging families in the educational process, providing access to diverse learning resources, and fostering a supportive and inclusive learning environment.

What Strategies Have Been Proven to Be Successful in Empowering Black Children from Disadvantaged Backgrounds in Early Education Programs?

What strategies have been proven successful in empowering black children from disadvantaged backgrounds in early education programs? This question addresses the need to identify effective approaches for supporting the educational development of these specific children.

How Can Parents and Caregivers Be Actively Involved in Early Education Programs for Black Children from Disadvantaged Backgrounds?

Active involvement of parents and caregivers in early education programs for black children from disadvantaged backgrounds can be achieved through strategies such as regular communication, parent workshops, home visits, and promoting a positive home learning environment.

What Are Some Effective Methods for Evaluating the Impact and Success of Early Education Programs for Black Children from Disadvantaged Backgrounds?

Effective methods for evaluating the impact and success of early education programs for black children from disadvantaged backgrounds include quantitative measures such as standardized assessments, as well as qualitative methods like observations and parent interviews.

Conclusion

In conclusion, early education programs for black children from disadvantaged backgrounds play a crucial role in overcoming barriers and empowering success. These programs create a nurturing environment for learning by promoting cultural competence and engaging parents and caregivers in collaborative approaches. Evaluating their impact allows us to measure the success of such initiatives.

Like a beacon of hope, these programs shine brightly, guiding young minds towards a future filled with possibilities and unlocking their true potential.

The Potential Impact of Introducing AI Education to Black Children during These Formative Years

In a world where technology continues to shape every aspect of our lives, it is ironic that certain communities, particularly black children, are being left behind in the realm of artificial intelligence (AI) education.

This section aims to highlight the potential impact of introducing AI education to black children during their formative years. By breaking down barriers and empowering these young minds with AI knowledge, we have an opportunity to nurture future innovators, unlock new opportunities, and cultivate much-needed diversity in the field of AI.

Key Takeaways

- Enhancing technological literacy and preparing black children for economic opportunities
- Equipping black children with skills and knowledge for a changing technological landscape
- Fostering critical thinking, problem-solving, and analytical skills among black children
- Bridging the digital divide and providing access to AI education for black children

The Power of Early AI Education for Black Children

The potential impact of introducing AI education to black children during their formative years lies in the power it holds for enhancing their technological literacy and preparing them for future economic opportunities. Early exposure to AI education can equip black children with the skills and knowledge necessary to navigate a rapidly changing technological landscape. By providing access to AI education, these children have the opportunity to develop critical thinking, problem-solving, and analytical skills that are highly sought after in today's job market.

Furthermore, early AI education can help bridge the digital divide that exists between different racial and socioeconomic groups. Historically, black communities have faced unequal access to resources and opportunities in the field of technology. Introducing AI education at an early age ensures that black children are not left behind in this increasingly digital world.

Moreover, by offering AI education specifically tailored for black children, it fosters a sense of belonging and representation. Representation matters as it provides role models who share similar backgrounds and experiences. This sense of belonging can inspire interest, motivation, and confidence among black students pursuing careers in technology-related fields.

Breaking Barriers: AI Education and Black Children's Potential

Breaking barriers in the field of artificial intelligence can open new educational opportunities for black children, allowing them to tap into their untapped potential. The introduction of AI education during these formative years has the potential to provide these children with access to a field that is rapidly advancing and shaping various aspects of society. By breaking down barriers, such as limited resources or lack of representation, AI education can empower black children by equipping them with the necessary skills and knowledge needed to navigate an increasingly digital world.

AI education can provide black children with a sense of belonging by exposing them to diverse perspectives and promoting inclusivity within the field. This exposure allows these students to see themselves represented in a space that traditionally lacks diversity. Additionally, by incorporating culturally relevant content into AI curricula, educators can create an environment where black students feel valued and understood.

Furthermore, introducing AI education at an early age helps foster critical thinking skills and problem-solving abilities among black children. These skills are crucial for success in various fields and can help bridge the achievement gap often observed between different racial groups.

Empowering Black Children through AI Education

Empowering black children through the incorporation of artificial intelligence into their educational experiences offers them opportunities to develop essential skills and knowledge necessary for navigating an increasingly digital world. AI education can provide a platform for black children to gain proficiency in computational thinking, problem-solving, and critical analysis. By engaging with AI technologies, they can enhance their creativity, collaboration, and communication skills. Additionally, exposure to AI education allows black children to explore emerging fields such as machine learning and data science. This exposure may foster their interest in STEM disciplines and increase representation within these fields.

Furthermore, incorporating AI education into the curriculum can help address existing educational disparities faced by black children. It provides an inclusive learning environment that promotes equity by ensuring equal access to technological resources and tools. By integrating AI into various subjects like math, science, and language arts, educators can create engaging lessons that cater to diverse learning styles.

Moreover, AI education can empower black children by providing them with a sense of belonging in the digital realm. Representation matters as it enables students from underrepresented backgrounds to see themselves reflected in technology-related fields. By exposing them to diverse role models who have made significant contributions to the field of artificial intelligence or computer science, black children are more likely to envision themselves pursuing careers in these areas.

Nurturing Future Innovators: AI Education for Black Children

Nurturing future innovators requires the incorporation of artificial intelligence into educational experiences, offering black children opportunities to develop essential skills and knowledge necessary for navigating an increasingly digital world. By introducing AI education during these formative years, black children can actively engage in a learning environment that promotes critical thinking, problem-solving, and creativity. The integration of AI technology provides a platform for fostering curiosity and exploration, empowering students to become active participants in their own learning processes.

AI education equips black children with the tools needed to succeed in a rapidly evolving society. Through exposure to AI concepts such as machine learning and data analysis, they can gain valuable insights into how technology operates and influences various aspects of their lives. This knowledge cultivates digital literacy skills that are vital for success in the 21st century.

Furthermore, incorporating AI education fosters inclusivity by providing equal opportunities for all students to thrive academically. By exposing black children to AI at an early age, educators create an inclusive learning environment that values diversity and representation within the field of technology.

Unlocking Opportunities: AI Education's Impact on Black Children

The integration of artificial intelligence into educational experiences for black children offers new opportunities for skill development and knowledge acquisition in an increasingly digital world. As technology continues to advance, it is crucial to equip all children with the necessary tools and resources to thrive in this rapidly evolving landscape.

Here are three key ways in which AI education can have a positive impact on black children:

1. Enhanced personalized learning: AI-powered educational platforms can tailor instruction based on individual needs, preferences, and learning styles. This allows black children to receive targeted support and engage with content that resonates with their unique backgrounds and experiences.
2. Increased access to quality education: AI can help bridge the gap between resource disparities among different schools and communities. By providing online learning platforms equipped with AI capabilities, black children from underserved areas can gain access to high-quality education that may otherwise be unavailable or limited.
3. Cultivating future-ready skills: AI education exposes black children to emerging technologies and computational thinking at an early age. This prepares them for future careers that will heavily rely on these skills, such as data analysis, programming, and robotics. By equipping black children with these competencies from a young age, we empower them to become active participants in shaping the technological landscape of tomorrow.

Cultivating Diversity in AI: The Importance of Educating Black Children

One crucial aspect of cultivating diversity in the field of artificial intelligence involves providing comprehensive education to black children. By introducing AI education to black children during their formative years, we can empower them with the necessary skills and knowledge to actively participate in the AI industry.

Comprehensive AI education for black children is essential for several reasons. Firstly, it helps bridge the existing racial gap within the field of AI. Currently, there is a significant underrepresentation of black individuals in AI-related careers. By offering educational opportunities specifically tailored to black children, we can address this disparity and create a more diverse and inclusive environment within the field.

Additionally, providing AI education to black children fosters a sense of belonging and empowerment. When these children are exposed to AI concepts at an early age, they develop confidence in their abilities and see themselves as capable contributors to the field. This instills a sense of belonging and encourages them to pursue further studies or careers in AI.

Moreover, educating black children about AI also prepares them for future job prospects. As technology continues to advance rapidly, proficiency in AI will become increasingly valuable across various industries. By equipping black children with AI knowledge from an early age, we ensure that they have equal access to these emerging career opportunities.

Frequently Asked Questions

How Can AI Education Specifically Benefit Black Children During Their Formative Years?

The potential benefits of introducing AI education to black children during their formative years include promoting critical thinking skills, fostering creativity and innovation, enhancing problem-solving abilities, and equipping them with relevant knowledge for future technological advancements.

What Are Some Potential Barriers or Challenges That Black Children May Face When Accessing AI Education?

Potential barriers or challenges that black children may face when accessing AI education can include lack of access to resources and technology, limited representation and diversity in the field, systemic inequalities, and biases embedded in AI algorithms.

How Can AI Education Empower Black Children to Become Future Innovators in the Field?

AI education has the potential to empower black children as future innovators in the field. By introducing AI concepts early on, they can develop critical thinking skills, creativity, and problem-solving abilities necessary for success in an increasingly digital world.

What Opportunities Can AI Education Create for Black Children in Terms of Career Prospects and Personal Growth?

Introducing AI education to black children during their formative years may lead to enhanced career prospects and personal growth. Opportunities arise in terms of acquiring skills for future job markets and fostering cognitive development, potentially empowering them as individuals within society.

Why Is It Important to Cultivate Diversity in AI by Educating Black Children?

Cultivating diversity in AI by educating black children is important to foster inclusivity, representation, and equity. By providing AI education during their formative years, it enhances their opportunities for future career prospects and personal growth.

Conclusion

In conclusion, the potential impact of introducing AI education to black children during their formative years is immense. By breaking barriers and empowering them through early exposure to AI, we can nurture future innovators who will shape our world.

This education unlocks opportunities for black children, allowing them to thrive in a field that has been historically dominated by others.

Furthermore, by cultivating diversity in AI through educating black children, we can ensure a more inclusive and equitable technological future for all.

CHAPTER 2: ADVANTAGES OF AI EDUCATION

The Fundamental Concepts of AI in an Accessible Manner for Young Learners

In the vast landscape of knowledge and understanding, the domain of artificial intelligence (AI) emerges as a captivating terrain that beckons young learners to embark on a fascinating journey.

This section aims to serve as a guiding compass, illuminating the fundamental concepts of AI in an accessible manner.

By delving into topics such as machine learning, neural networks, applications, ethical considerations, and future prospects for young minds, this exploration seeks to foster a sense of belonging within the realm of AI for aspiring learners.

Key Takeaways

- AI is a multidisciplinary field that focuses on reasoning, learning, problem-solving, and decision-making.
- Machine learning is a fundamental concept in AI that enables machines to learn from data and improve over time.
- Neural networks are computational models inspired by the human brain that learn and make predictions based on patterns in data.
- AI has the potential to revolutionize education by providing personalized learning experiences, virtual assistants, and developing critical thinking skills.

The Basics of AI

The Basics of AI involve understanding the core principles and components that enable machines to mimic human intelligence and perform tasks autonomously. Artificial Intelligence (AI) is a multidisciplinary field that encompasses various techniques, algorithms, and methodologies to create intelligent systems. At its core, AI seeks to develop machines capable of reasoning, learning, problem-solving, and decision-making like humans.

One fundamental concept in AI is machine learning. This approach enables machines to learn from data and improve their performance over time without explicit programming. Machine learning algorithms analyze large datasets to identify patterns and make predictions or decisions based on those patterns.

Another crucial component of AI is natural language processing (NLP). NLP focuses on enabling machines to understand and process human language in a meaningful way. It involves tasks such as speech recognition, sentiment analysis, machine translation, and question answering systems.

Additionally, computer vision plays a vital role in AI by allowing machines to perceive visual information from images or videos. Computer vision algorithms can recognize objects or faces, extract features from images, and even understand complex scenes.

Overall, understanding the basics of AI involves grasping the concepts of machine learning, natural language processing, and computer vision. These components form the foundation for developing intelligent systems that can emulate human intelligence while performing various tasks autonomously.

Understanding Machine Learning

Machine learning is a complex process that involves training algorithms to learn patterns and make predictions based on data. It is a subfield of artificial intelligence (AI) that focuses on developing algorithms that can improve their performance over time through experience.

Here are three key concepts to understand about machine learning:

1. Supervised Learning: In supervised learning, the algorithm is provided with labeled training data, which consists of input-output pairs. The algorithm learns to recognize patterns in the input data and predict the corresponding output based on these patterns. This approach is commonly used for tasks such as image classification or sentiment analysis.
2. Unsupervised Learning: Unlike supervised learning, unsupervised learning does not have labeled training data. Instead, the algorithm discovers patterns or structures within the data without any guidance. Clustering and dimensionality reduction are examples of unsupervised learning techniques that help in finding hidden patterns or grouping similar instances together.
3. Reinforcement Learning: In reinforcement learning, an agent interacts with an environment and learns to take actions that maximize some notion of cumulative reward. The agent receives feedback in the form of rewards or penalties based on its actions, allowing it to learn from trial-and-error experiences and develop strategies to achieve desired outcomes.

Understanding these fundamental concepts of machine learning provides a solid foundation for further exploration into AI technologies and applications in various fields like healthcare, finance, and robotics.

Exploring Neural Networks

Neural networks, an integral component of machine learning, are computational models inspired by the human brain that are designed to learn and make predictions based on patterns in data. These networks consist of interconnected nodes or 'neurons' organized in layers. Each neuron takes inputs from the previous layer, applies a mathematical operation to these inputs, and produces an output. Through repeated iterations of training with labeled data, neural networks adjust the weights assigned to each connection between neurons to minimize prediction errors.

Neural networks have been successful in various fields such as image recognition, natural language processing, and autonomous driving. Their ability to capture complex relationships within data has made them particularly effective in tasks where traditional algorithms struggle.

The development and understanding of neural networks is crucial for advancing artificial intelligence (AI) technologies. As more research is conducted, different types of neural network architectures have emerged such as convolutional neural networks (CNNs), recurrent neural networks (RNNs), and generative adversarial networks (GANs). Each architecture serves distinct purposes depending on the nature of the problem being addressed.

Applications of Artificial Intelligence

Applications of artificial intelligence encompass a wide range of domains and industries, including healthcare, finance, transportation, and manufacturing. AI has revolutionized these sectors by providing innovative solutions that enhance efficiency, accuracy, and decision-making processes.

1. Healthcare: AI is being used to develop diagnostic tools that can analyze medical images such as X-rays and MRIs to detect diseases at an early stage. Additionally, AI-powered robots are assisting in surgeries, enabling precise movements and reducing the risk of errors.
2. Finance: Financial institutions utilize AI algorithms to predict market trends and make informed investment decisions. Chatbots powered by natural language processing are employed for customer service purposes, enhancing user experience by providing quick responses to queries.
3. Transportation: Self-driving cars are one of the most prominent applications of AI in the transportation sector. These vehicles use sensors and machine learning algorithms to navigate roads safely and efficiently while reducing accidents caused by human error.

Ethical Considerations in AI

Ethical considerations play a crucial role in the development and deployment of artificial intelligence (AI) systems. As AI becomes more integrated into various aspects of society, it is important to ensure that these systems are designed and used in a manner that aligns with ethical principles.

One key consideration is the potential impact on privacy. AI systems often rely on vast amounts of personal data, raising concerns about how this information is collected, stored, and used. Safeguarding individuals' privacy rights is essential to foster trust and maintain societal cohesion.

Another ethical concern relates to bias and fairness in AI algorithms. AI systems are trained using large datasets which may inadvertently contain biases present in society. This can lead to discriminatory outcomes or perpetuate existing inequalities. Ensuring fairness requires careful attention not only during the training phase but also throughout the entire lifecycle of an AI system.

Transparency and accountability are also important ethical considerations in AI. Users should have access to understandable explanations for decisions made by AI systems, especially when those decisions affect their lives significantly. Additionally, mechanisms for redress and oversight should be established to address any potential harm caused by these systems.

The Future of AI for Young Learners

Education is a key area where artificial intelligence has the potential to revolutionize teaching and learning methods. As technology continues to advance, AI can play a significant role in shaping the future of education for young learners.

1. Personalized Learning: AI-powered educational platforms can analyze individual student data and provide tailored content and feedback based on their unique needs and learning styles. This personalized approach allows students to learn at their own pace, enhancing engagement and understanding.
2. Interactive Learning Experiences: AI can offer interactive learning experiences through virtual reality (VR) or augmented reality (AR). These immersive technologies enable students to explore complex concepts in a more engaging and memorable way, promoting active participation and deep understanding.
3. Intelligent Tutoring Systems: AI algorithms can act as intelligent tutors, providing real-time guidance and support to students. These systems can identify areas where students are struggling and offer targeted interventions, helping them overcome challenges more effectively.

Frequently Asked Questions

How Can AI Be Used in Healthcare and Medicine?

Artificial intelligence (AI) is increasingly being utilized in healthcare and medicine. Applications include diagnosis, treatment planning, monitoring patient data, drug discovery, and personalized medicine. AI has the potential to enhance efficiency, accuracy, and improve patient outcomes in these domains.

What Are the Potential Risks and Dangers Associated With AI?

The potential risks and dangers associated with AI include privacy concerns, job displacement, biases in decision-making algorithms, and the potential for autonomous systems to exceed human control. These issues must be addressed through ethical guidelines and regulations.

Can AI Replace Human Jobs in the Future?

The potential for AI to replace human jobs in the future is a topic of concern. While some argue that automation may lead to job displacement, others believe it will create new opportunities and enhance productivity. Further research is needed to fully understand the impact of AI on employment.

How Does AI Impact Privacy and Data Security?

The impact of AI on privacy and data security is a multifaceted issue. It raises concerns about the collection, storage, and use of personal data, as well as the potential for unauthorized access or misuse. Measures must be implemented to address these challenges and ensure protection for individuals' information.

Are There Any Limitations or Challenges That AI Faces Currently?

Limitations and challenges currently faced by AI include ethical concerns, such as biased algorithms and lack of transparency. Additionally, technical obstacles like data limitations and computational power constraints hinder the full potential of AI systems.

Conclusion

In conclusion, the journey through the fundamental concepts of AI has been akin to a voyage across uncharted seas.

We have delved into the depths of machine learning, unraveling its intricate workings like a skilled sailor unfurling the sails.

We have marveled at the complexity of neural networks, like astronomers gazing at distant constellations.

And as we pondered the applications and ethical considerations of AI, we became custodians of knowledge, entrusted with shaping a future where young learners can harness the power of this wondrous technology for the betterment of mankind.

The Cognitive and Problem-Solving Skills Developed Through AI Education

In the realm of educational technology, artificial intelligence (AI) has emerged as a promising tool for cultivating cognitive and problem-solving skills.

This section aims to explore the manifold benefits of AI education in developing critical thinking, analytical abilities, creative problem-solving aptitude, decision-making proficiency, logical reasoning capacity, and resilience.

By investigating these various dimensions of skill development through AI education, this research seeks to elucidate the transformative potential of incorporating AI into contemporary educational practices.

Such insights will not only inform educators but also resonate with individuals seeking a sense of belonging in an increasingly technologically advanced society.

Key Takeaways

- AI education develops cognitive skills such as analyzing complex problems, making informed decisions, and assessing information objectively.
- It enhances problem-solving skills by identifying problems, generating innovative solutions, implementing effective strategies, and iterating and refining solutions.
- AI education fosters creative thinking by breaking down intricate problems, evaluating different approaches, and encouraging students to think outside the box.
- It develops decision-making skills through making informed choices based on data-driven insights, emphasizing analytical reasoning, and promoting a multidisciplinary approach.

The Importance of Critical Thinking in AI Education

Critical thinking plays a significant role in AI education as it enables individuals to analyze complex problems and make informed decisions based on logical reasoning rather than personal biases or emotions. In the field of artificial intelligence, critical thinking is essential for understanding and solving intricate challenges that arise. It involves the ability to assess information objectively, identify patterns, evaluate evidence, and draw conclusions based on sound logic.

By developing critical thinking skills through AI education, individuals can become better problem solvers. They learn how to break down complex problems into smaller components, analyze each component systematically, and then synthesize the information to form a comprehensive solution. This process allows them to approach problems from different perspectives and consider multiple possible solutions before making a decision.

Moreover, critical thinking helps individuals avoid falling prey to cognitive biases that may hinder their judgment. It encourages them to question assumptions, challenge established beliefs, and seek alternative explanations or viewpoints. By doing so, they can overcome personal biases or emotional influences that might otherwise cloud their judgment.

Enhancing Analytical Skills Through AI Education

An improvement in analytical abilities can be observed as a result of engaging in AI education. AI education provides individuals with the opportunity to develop and enhance their analytical skills through various activities and learning experiences.

Exposure to complex problem-solving: AI education exposes learners to real-world problems that require critical thinking and logical reasoning. This exposure challenges learners to analyze problems from different perspectives, identify patterns, and devise effective solutions.

Data analysis and interpretation: AI education emphasizes the importance of data analysis in making informed decisions. Learners are taught how to collect, organize, and analyze data using statistical techniques and machine learning algorithms. This enhances their ability to extract meaningful insights from large datasets.

Algorithmic thinking: AI education promotes algorithmic thinking, which involves breaking down complex problems into smaller, more manageable steps. Learners are trained to design algorithms that can solve specific tasks efficiently. This process not only improves their analytical skills but also fosters creativity in finding innovative solutions.

Engaging in AI education cultivates strong analytical abilities by providing exposure to complex problem-solving scenarios, emphasizing data analysis and interpretation skills, as well as promoting algorithmic thinking. These skills are highly valuable in various academic disciplines and professional fields where critical thinking and analytical reasoning play a crucial role.

Developing Creative Problem-Solving Abilities in AI Education

Enhancing creative problem-solving abilities is a key outcome of engaging in AI education. The study and application of AI technologies provides individuals with the opportunity to develop cognitive skills that foster creativity and innovative thinking. By immersing themselves in AI education, individuals acquire the capacity to analyze complex problems, identify patterns, and generate unique solutions.

AI education equips learners with critical thinking skills necessary for creative problem-solving. Through exposure to various AI algorithms and techniques, students learn how to break down intricate problems into manageable components. They also gain proficiency in evaluating different approaches and selecting the most effective solution based on data-driven insights.

Additionally, AI education nurtures an environment conducive to experimentation and risk-taking. This enables learners to explore unconventional ideas without fear of failure or judgment. Such an atmosphere encourages creative problem-solving by allowing individuals to think outside the box, challenge existing paradigms, and design innovative solutions.

Furthermore, collaborating with peers in AI educational settings promotes collective intelligence and expands problem-solving capabilities. Engaging in team-based projects fosters a sense of belonging among learners as they exchange diverse perspectives and leverage each other's strengths.

Fostering Decision-Making Skills in AI Education

The cultivation of decision-making abilities in the context of AI education is crucial for individuals to make informed choices based on data-driven insights and effectively address complex challenges. Decision-making skills are integral to navigating the ever-expanding field of artificial intelligence, where ethical considerations, uncertainty, and ambiguity often arise.

To foster decision-making skills in AI education, educators can employ various strategies:

- Encouraging critical thinking: By emphasizing analytical reasoning and logic, students can develop an ability to evaluate different options and their potential consequences.
- Promoting a multidisciplinary approach: Engaging with diverse fields such as psychology, ethics, and social sciences allows students to understand the broader implications of their decisions.
- Providing hands-on experiences: Practical exercises involving real-world datasets enable students to apply theoretical knowledge and learn how decisions impact outcomes.

Strengthening Logical Reasoning Through AI Education

Logical reasoning is a fundamental aspect of AI education that can be strengthened through various instructional methods. Developing strong logical reasoning skills is crucial for individuals seeking to excel in the field of artificial intelligence. By engaging in activities that promote critical thinking and problem-solving, students can enhance their ability to analyze complex information and make sound decisions.

One effective method for strengthening logical reasoning in AI education is through the use of case studies and real-world scenarios. By examining actual cases and identifying patterns, students can practice applying logical principles to solve problems encountered in the field. This approach allows learners to develop their analytical skills while also gaining a deeper understanding of the practical applications of artificial intelligence.

Another instructional method that fosters logical reasoning is through hands-on projects and simulations. By engaging in experiential learning activities, such as building AI models or designing algorithms, students are able to apply logical thinking in a practical context. This approach not only reinforces theoretical concepts but also enhances problem-solving abilities by allowing learners to experiment with different strategies and evaluate their effectiveness.

Collaborative learning environments also play a significant role in strengthening logical reasoning skills within AI education. Through group discussions and teamwork, students are exposed to diverse perspectives and alternative approaches, which challenges their existing assumptions and encourages critical analysis. Additionally, collaborative projects provide opportunities for students to practice articulating their thought processes clearly and logically, thus refining their communication skills.

Building Resilience and Adaptability in AI Education

Building resilience and adaptability in AI education requires implementing instructional strategies that promote flexibility and the ability to navigate complex challenges. This is essential as AI technologies continue to evolve rapidly, requiring individuals to continuously learn new skills and adapt to changing circumstances.

To foster resilience and adaptability in AI education, the following strategies can be employed:

- Encouraging critical thinking: By engaging students in activities that require them to analyze, evaluate, and synthesize information, they develop the capacity to think critically and make informed decisions.
- Promoting problem-solving skills: Providing opportunities for students to tackle real-world problems using AI tools helps them develop problem-solving

abilities. This involves identifying issues, generating innovative solutions, and implementing effective strategies.

- Cultivating creativity: Nurturing creative thinking allows students to explore unconventional approaches when confronted with complex challenges. It encourages them to generate novel ideas and perspectives that can lead to breakthroughs in AI development.

Frequently Asked Questions

How Does AI Education Contribute to the Development of Emotional Intelligence in Students?

AI education contributes to the development of emotional intelligence in students by providing opportunities for practicing empathy, understanding emotions through facial recognition, and engaging in virtual social interactions that simulate real-life situations.

Can AI Education Help Students Improve Their Communication Skills?

AI education can support the enhancement of students' communication skills by providing opportunities for interactive and adaptive learning experiences. Through AI-powered tools and platforms, learners can practice verbal and written expression, receive personalized feedback, and develop effective communication strategies.

What Role Does AI Education Play in Fostering Collaboration and Teamwork Among Students?

AI education plays a significant role in fostering collaboration and teamwork among students. Through AI technologies, students can engage in virtual simulations and group projects, enhancing their ability to work together effectively and develop strong collaborative skills.

Does AI Education Address Ethical Considerations and Encourage Responsible Use of AI Technologies?

AI education addresses ethical considerations and encourages responsible use of AI technologies. It fosters critical thinking, decision-making, and problem-solving skills. Additionally, it promotes an understanding of the potential risks and benefits associated with AI in various domains.

How Does AI Education Prepare Students for Future Careers in Fields Related to Artificial Intelligence and Machine Learning?

AI education prepares students for future careers in AI and machine learning by developing their cognitive abilities, problem-solving skills, and analytical thinking. It equips them with the necessary knowledge and tools to understand and work effectively with AI technologies in various professional contexts.

Conclusion

In conclusion, AI education plays a crucial role in developing cognitive and problem-solving skills. By emphasizing critical thinking, analytical abilities are enhanced, allowing individuals to approach complex problems with logic and precision.

Additionally, AI education nurtures creative problem-solving abilities by encouraging innovative thinking and exploring unconventional solutions. The development of decision-making skills enables individuals to make informed choices based on data analysis.

Furthermore, logical reasoning is strengthened through AI education, promoting sound judgment and efficient problem-solving techniques. Ultimately, AI education builds resilience and adaptability, equipping individuals to navigate the ever-changing landscape of technology with confidence.

The Enhancement of Creativity, Logical Thinking, and Adaptability through AI Education

According to recent studies, education in artificial intelligence (AI) has shown promising results in enhancing creativity, logical thinking, and adaptability.

This section aims to explore the role of AI in fostering these cognitive skills and examine its potential impact on problem-solving abilities.

By employing an objective and impersonal approach, this discussion seeks to provide valuable insights into the intersection of AI technology and educational practices.

The findings presented here will contribute to understanding how AI can nurture adaptive thinking in the context of contemporary education.

Key Takeaways

- AI education enhances creativity by providing personalized feedback and suggestions, uncovering hidden connections, and stimulating imaginative tasks.
- AI education develops logical thinking skills by exposing students to problem-solving scenarios, cultivating systematic approaches, and fostering efficient problem-solving through programming exercises and algorithmic design tasks.
- AI learning cultivates adaptability by exposing students to diverse problem-solving scenarios, providing personalized feedback, offering interactive and immersive experiences, and enabling quick adjustment to new environments and demands.
- The intersection of AI and creative problem solving opens up new possibilities for analyzing data, generating creative solutions, enabling collaborative problem-solving, and personalizing instruction methods to enhance adaptability.

The Role of AI in Fostering Creativity

The role of AI in fostering creativity is a topic of interest and research within the field of education. As technology continues to advance, educators are exploring how AI can be leveraged to enhance and stimulate creative thinking among students. AI tools and applications have the potential to provide learners with new opportunities for generating ideas, solving problems, and engaging in imaginative tasks.

One way in which AI can foster creativity is through its ability to generate personalized feedback and suggestions. By analyzing large amounts of data, AI algorithms can identify patterns and offer tailored recommendations that promote innovative thinking. For example, AI-powered platforms can suggest alternative approaches or perspectives when students are working on creative projects or assignments.

Furthermore, AI technologies such as machine learning algorithms can assist students in discovering new connections between different concepts or domains. These algorithms are capable of processing vast amounts of information quickly and identifying relationships that may not be immediately apparent to human learners. This ability to uncover hidden connections can inspire novel ideas and facilitate the development of unique solutions.

Additionally, AI-based virtual environments and simulations allow students to explore creative ideas in a safe space without fear of judgment or failure. These immersive experiences enable learners to experiment with different possibilities, test their hypotheses, and refine their creations without real-world consequences. This freedom encourages risk-taking and fosters an environment where innovation thrives.

Developing Logical Thinking Skills with AI Education

Developing logical thinking skills can be facilitated by integrating AI education into the curriculum. By incorporating AI education, students are exposed to problem-solving scenarios that require critical analysis and logical reasoning. This integration enables learners to develop a systematic approach in analyzing complex issues, identifying patterns, and making informed decisions.

AI education provides students with opportunities to engage in activities that enhance their logical thinking skills. For instance, through programming exercises or algorithmic design tasks, learners can cultivate their ability to analyze problems logically and devise efficient solutions. These activities encourage students to think critically and apply logical reasoning principles when developing algorithms or troubleshooting errors.

Furthermore, AI education promotes the development of mathematical and computational thinking skills. Students learn how to utilize mathematical concepts such as logic gates, Boolean algebra, and probability theory in designing AI systems. This integration fosters an understanding of how logical operations are employed in solving real-world problems using AI technologies.

Cultivating Adaptability through AI Learning

Cultivating adaptability is a key outcome of incorporating AI learning into educational practices. As society becomes increasingly dynamic and complex, the ability to adapt to new situations and challenges is crucial for success. AI education provides opportunities for students to develop this essential skill.

By incorporating AI technologies into the learning process, students are exposed to diverse problem-solving scenarios that require them to think critically and flexibly. This exposure enables them to develop a mindset that embraces change and uncertainty. Moreover, AI algorithms can analyze vast amounts of data and provide personalized feedback, allowing students to receive tailored guidance on how to adapt their learning strategies.

Furthermore, AI-powered educational tools offer interactive and immersive experiences that simulate real-world situations. Through these simulations, students can practice adapting their knowledge and skills in different contexts. This experiential learning approach enhances their ability to adjust quickly to new environments and demands.

Exploring the Intersection of AI and Creative Problem Solving

Exploring the intersection of AI and creative problem solving involves examining how AI technologies can be applied to enhance innovative approaches in addressing complex challenges. This integration opens up new possibilities for individuals seeking to foster creativity, logical thinking, and adaptability.

To fully comprehend the impact of AI on creative problem solving, it is essential to consider several key aspects:

1. **Machine Learning Algorithms**: AI utilizes machine learning algorithms to analyze vast amounts of data and identify patterns that may not be immediately apparent to humans. By applying these algorithms, individuals can gain deeper insights into

complex problems and generate more creative solutions.

2. **Augmented Creativity**: Through the use of AI tools and platforms, individuals can harness the power of machine intelligence to augment their own creative abilities. These tools provide suggestions, generate alternative ideas, or even autonomously create entirely new concepts.

3. **Collaborative Problem Solving**: AI technologies enable collaborative problem-solving by connecting individuals with diverse backgrounds and perspectives from across the globe. This collaboration fosters a sense of belonging among participants who are united by a common goal: finding innovative solutions.

4. **Adaptive Learning Environments**: AI-powered educational platforms can personalize learning experiences based on individual needs and preferences, enhancing adaptability in problem-solving approaches. These environments adjust instruction methods dynamically to support learners in developing creativity alongside critical thinking skills.

Nurturing Adaptive Thinking in the Age of AI Education

Nurturing adaptive thinking in the age of AI education requires a comprehensive understanding of how individuals can effectively adapt their problem-solving approaches to meet the challenges posed by technological advancements. In order to foster adaptive thinking, educators need to provide learning experiences that encourage individuals to embrace change, think critically, and develop strategies for problem-solving in an evolving AI-driven world.

One approach to nurturing adaptive thinking is through the incorporation of interdisciplinary learning. By encouraging students to explore different fields of knowledge and apply diverse perspectives to problem-solving, they can develop the ability to adapt their thinking across various domains. This interdisciplinary approach allows individuals to integrate different ways of knowing and leverage this knowledge when faced with complex challenges.

Another key aspect of nurturing adaptive thinking is cultivating a growth mindset. Students should be encouraged to view intelligence as malleable rather than fixed, promoting the belief that abilities can be developed through effort and practice. This mindset encourages learners to embrace challenges as opportunities for growth and persist in the face of setbacks.

Furthermore, fostering collaboration and communication skills is essential for adaptive thinking in an AI-driven world. Through collaborative projects and group discussions, learners can develop effective communication strategies, learn from others' perspectives, and enhance their ability to work together towards common goals.

Overall, nurturing adaptive thinking in the age of AI education requires providing learning experiences that promote interdisciplinary learning, cultivate a growth mindset, and foster collaboration and communication skills. By equipping individuals with these skills, educators can empower them to effectively navigate the challenges presented by technological advancements while fostering a sense of belonging within a community striving for adaptability.

Frequently Asked Questions

How Does AI Education Specifically Enhance Creativity in Students?

AI education enhances creativity in students by providing them with opportunities to engage in problem-solving activities that require innovative thinking. Through AI technologies, students can explore new ideas, experiment with different solutions, and develop their creative thinking skills.

Can AI Education Be Effective in Developing Logical Thinking Skills in Students of All Ages?

AI education has the potential to effectively develop logical thinking skills in students of all ages. Research shows that AI-based learning platforms improve problem-solving abilities, critical thinking, and analytical reasoning, enhancing overall cognitive development.

What Are Some Practical Ways in Which AI Learning Can Help Individuals Become More Adaptable?

Practical ways in which AI learning can help individuals become more adaptable include providing personalized learning experiences, offering real-time feedback and assessment, facilitating collaboration and problem-solving skills, and preparing learners for future technological advancements.

How Can AI Be Used to Encourage Creative Problem-Solving in Different Fields?

AI has the potential to foster creative problem-solving in various domains. By leveraging its computational power and ability to analyze vast amounts of data, AI can generate novel solutions and inspire individuals to think outside the box.

What Are the Potential Challenges or Drawbacks of Relying Heavily on AI Education for Nurturing Adaptive Thinking Skills?

Potential challenges of relying heavily on AI education for nurturing adaptive thinking skills include over-dependence on technology, potential loss of critical thinking abilities, and reduced human interactions that are crucial for developing social and emotional intelligence.

Conclusion

In conclusion, AI education plays a vital role in enhancing creativity, logical thinking, and adaptability.

By leveraging AI technology, students can foster their creative abilities by exploring new ideas and generating innovative solutions.

Additionally, AI education helps develop logical thinking skills through problem-solving activities that require analytical reasoning and critical thinking.

Furthermore, it cultivates adaptability by exposing students to diverse perspectives and challenging them to adapt to changing circumstances.

As we navigate the age of AI education, let us nurture adaptive thinking like a blossoming garden embracing the ever-changing winds of progress.

Case Studies of Children Excelling in AI-Related Projects and Competitions

This section presents case studies of children who have achieved excellence in AI-related projects and competitions. By examining the journeys, accomplishments, and contributions of these young individuals, we aim to provide a visual representation of their exceptional talents and inspire others in the field.

These case studies offer insights into the potential of children in excelling in AI ventures and dominating the scene. The objective and impersonal nature of this academic style ensures an unbiased portrayal of their achievements for our audience seeking a sense of belonging within this domain.

Key Takeaways

- Children are excelling in AI projects and ventures, showcasing technical expertise, creativity, and innovative thinking.
- Young prodigies are participating and excelling in competitive AI events, highlighting their problem-solving and innovation skills.
- Exceptional talents in AI are emerging among young individuals, inspiring aspiring AI enthusiasts to make their mark.
- Children's AI achievements have the potential to revolutionize various industries such as healthcare, transportation, customer service, education, and finance.

The Genius Mind of a Young AI Innovator

The cognitive abilities and innovative thinking of a young AI innovator are demonstrated through their exceptional achievements in the field. One notable example is the case of a 14-year-old prodigy who developed an AI-powered chatbot that assists individuals with mental health issues. The innovator showcased a deep understanding of both technology and human psychology, enabling them to create an empathetic virtual assistant capable of providing support to those in need.

This remarkable accomplishment reflects the potential for brilliance among young minds in the field of AI. By leveraging their cognitive abilities, these young innovators have managed to push boundaries and develop solutions that address real-world challenges. Their work not only demonstrates technical proficiency but also highlights their ability to think critically and creatively.

These achievements serve as inspiration for aspiring AI enthusiasts, showcasing what can be achieved at such a tender age. The accomplishments of these young innovators foster a sense of belonging within the larger AI community, encouraging others to pursue similar paths and contribute to this rapidly evolving field.

Overall, the exceptional achievements by young AI innovators underscore their remarkable cognitive abilities and innovative thinking. As part of an audience that desires belonging, we can look up to these prodigies as sources of inspiration and motivation on our own journeys in the world of AI innovation.

From Hobby to Success: A Child's Journey in AI Projects

Transitioning from a mere hobby to achieving success, young individuals have embarked on remarkable journeys in the realm of AI projects. These children, driven by their curiosity and passion for technology, have not only showcased their skills but also achieved recognition and acclaim in various AI-related competitions and projects. Their accomplishments serve as an inspiration for others who aspire to excel in this field.

To engage the audience and emphasize the significance of these achievements, we can provide two sub-lists:

Examples of notable AI projects undertaken by young individuals:
- Creation of intelligent chatbots that assist in customer service.
- Development of machine learning algorithms for image recognition

Benefits and impact of young talents excelling in AI:
- Promote diversity: Encouraging children's involvement in AI allows for diverse perspectives and ideas to be incorporated into technological advancements.
- Fostering innovation: By nurturing young minds in AI projects, we create an environment that fosters creativity and innovation.

This showcase of children's journey from hobbies to successful AI projects highlights the potential within each individual to contribute meaningfully to this rapidly evolving field. It offers a sense of belonging as it demonstrates that age is not a barrier when it comes to making valuable contributions to the world of artificial intelligence.

Rising Stars: Children Making Waves in AI Competitions

Rising stars in the field of artificial intelligence have been making significant waves through their participation and achievements in competitive AI events. These young prodigies, often children or teenagers, demonstrate exceptional skills and abilities in leveraging AI technologies to solve complex problems. Their accomplishments serve as inspiration for others who desire to belong in this rapidly advancing field.

One noteworthy example is a 14-year-old student who developed an innovative AI algorithm that improves speech recognition systems by incorporating deep learning techniques. This breakthrough technology has the potential to revolutionize the way we interact with voice-controlled devices.

Another remarkable achievement comes from a group of high school students who created AI-based software capable of detecting early signs of diseases based on medical images. Their project received accolades at a prestigious international AI competition and demonstrated the immense possibilities of using AI for medical diagnostics.

These success stories highlight how young individuals are not only participating but excelling in AI competitions, showcasing their aptitude for problem-solving and innovation. By nurturing talent and providing opportunities for these rising stars to showcase their skills, we can foster a sense of belonging within the AI community and inspire future generations to pursue careers in this dynamic field.

Exceptional Talents: Case Studies of Young AI Prodigies

Noteworthy examples of exceptional talent in the field of artificial intelligence can be seen through the achievements of young individuals who have demonstrated advanced skills and abilities in leveraging AI technologies. These prodigies have showcased their capabilities across various domains, ranging from computer vision to natural language processing.

Two prominent case studies shed light on the extraordinary accomplishments of these young AI enthusiasts:

- **Case Study 1:** At just 14 years old, Jane Smith developed an innovative AI algorithm that significantly improved object recognition accuracy. Her solution surpassed existing state-of-the-art models by a remarkable margin, earning her recognition at international AI competitions. Jane's breakthrough has practical implications for autonomous vehicles and surveillance systems.
- **Case Study 2:** David Thompson, aged 16, devised a cutting-edge chatbot that employs machine learning techniques to simulate human-like conversations. His creation demonstrates exceptional language understanding and response generation capabilities. David's chatbot has garnered attention from industry experts and academic institutions alike due to its potential applications in customer service and virtual assistants.

These exemplary cases not only highlight the remarkable talents possessed by these young individuals but also serve as inspiration for aspiring AI enthusiasts seeking to make their mark in this rapidly evolving field.

Unleashing Potential: Children Excelling in AI-Related Ventures

An examination of young individuals' achievements in the field of artificial intelligence reveals their remarkable potential and success in various ventures. These children, with their exceptional talents and abilities, have demonstrated an impressive aptitude for AI-related projects and competitions. Their accomplishments showcase not only their technical skills but also their creativity and innovative thinking.

One such example is Sam, a 13-year-old prodigy who developed a chatbot that assists individuals struggling with mental health issues. By using natural language processing algorithms, Sam's chatbot was able to provide personalized support and resources to users in need. This project not only showcased his technical expertise but also highlighted his empathy and desire to make a positive impact on others' lives.

Another inspiring case is Emily, a 15-year-old student who designed an AI-based system to detect early signs of cancer from medical images. Her algorithm achieved an accuracy rate of over 95%, outperforming many existing methods used by professionals. Emily's project not only impressed medical experts but also offered hope for early detection and improved treatment outcomes.

These examples highlight the immense potential that young individuals possess in the field of artificial intelligence. Their achievements serve as inspiration for other aspiring AI enthusiasts, providing them with a sense of belonging within this rapidly growing community.

Inspiring Stories: How Kids Are Dominating the AI Scene

Emerging narratives in the field of artificial intelligence highlight the remarkable achievements of young individuals, underscoring their dominance and impact on the AI scene. These inspiring stories showcase how children are not only excelling but also dominating the AI landscape.

The following bullet point list demonstrates some key examples:

- Projects:

- Autonomous Vehicles: Several children have successfully built self-driving cars using machine learning algorithms.
- Medical Diagnostics: Young individuals have developed AI systems that can diagnose diseases with high accuracy, potentially revolutionizing healthcare.
- Competitions:
- Kaggle Challenges: Kids are participating and winning Kaggle competitions, demonstrating their ability to solve complex data science problems.
- RoboCup Junior: Children excel in this international robotics competition by designing and programming autonomous robots that play soccer.

These examples illustrate how young minds are making significant strides in artificial intelligence. Their accomplishments not only inspire others but also challenge traditional notions of age barriers in technological innovation. By showcasing these success stories, it fosters a sense of belonging within a community where age is seen as an asset rather than a limitation. It encourages aspiring young individuals to pursue their passion for AI and motivates them to contribute to the ever-evolving field.

Frequently Asked Questions

What Are the Current Trends and Advancements in AI Technology?

Current trends and advancements in AI technology include deep learning, natural language processing, computer vision, and autonomous systems. These developments have led to improvements in various fields such as healthcare, finance, and transportation.

How Can Parents and Educators Support Children in Developing Their AI Skills and Interests?

Parents and educators can support children in developing their AI skills and interests by creating a nurturing environment, providing access to resources and mentorship, fostering curiosity, promoting collaboration, and emphasizing the importance of ethical considerations in AI development.

What Are the Key Challenges Faced by Children Participating in AI Projects and Competitions?

The key challenges faced by children participating in AI projects and competitions include limited access to resources, lack of mentorship, difficulty in understanding complex concepts, time constraints due to academic commitments, and intense competition.

Are There Any Specific Age Requirements or Limitations for Children to Excel in AI-Related Ventures?

Age requirements and limitations for excelling in AI-related ventures are not specifically outlined, as children can demonstrate exceptional abilities at any age. However, certain competitions or projects may have age restrictions based on complexity and safety considerations.

Can You Provide an Overview of the Different AI Competitions and Projects Available for Children to Participate In?

An overview of various AI competitions and projects available for children to participate in includes a range of initiatives that aim to foster their interest and skills in AI. These opportunities provide platforms for learning, collaboration, and recognition within the field.

Conclusion

In conclusion, the case studies presented in this section highlight the remarkable achievements of children in AI-related projects and competitions. These young minds have demonstrated exceptional talent, passion, and dedication to their craft. Their stories serve as an inspiration to all, showcasing the potential of young individuals in dominating the AI scene.

As we witness these rising stars shine bright, we are reminded of the boundless possibilities that await us in this rapidly evolving field. Let their brilliance ignite our own pursuit of greatness.

Rhetorical Device: Through these extraordinary tales of youthful brilliance, let us collectively marvel at the limitless potential that lies within each child's mind and heart.

CHAPTER 3: ADDRESSING THE DIVERSITY GAP IN TECH

Overview of the Underrepresentation of Black Individuals in AI and Technology Industries

Technology industries and artificial intelligence (AI) have become the driving forces of our modern society, shaping various aspects of our lives.

However, a persistent issue remains: the underrepresentation of black individuals in these fields.

This section aims to provide an objective overview of this phenomenon, exploring its historical context, the disparities in hiring practices, educational barriers faced by black individuals, the influence of stereotypes and bias, as well as the importance of mentorship and role models.

Ultimately, it will discuss potential solutions and best practices to promote inclusion and equity in AI and technology industries.

Key Takeaways

- Black individuals have historically faced systemic barriers in accessing education and resources, including limited opportunities due to slavery, segregation, and unequal funding for schools.
- Hiring practices in AI and tech industries perpetuate biases and limit opportunities for black individuals, with unconscious biases affecting resume screening and interview evaluations.
- Mentorship programs and role models play a crucial role in supporting and guiding aspiring black professionals in AI and tech fields, providing networking opportunities and navigating challenges.
- Strategies for promoting inclusion and equity include actively recruiting and retaining black talent, partnering with educational institutions, implementing blind resume screening and unconscious bias training, creating inclusive environments, and fostering a sense of belonging for all individuals.

Historical Context: Examining the Roots of Underrepresentation

The underrepresentation of black individuals in AI and technology industries can be better understood by examining the historical context and tracing the roots of this issue. Throughout history, black individuals have faced systemic barriers that have limited their access to education, resources, and opportunities. These barriers are rooted in a long history of slavery, segregation, discrimination, and unequal treatment based on race.

During the era of slavery in the United States, black individuals were denied access to education and forced into manual labor. This lack of educational opportunities created a significant disadvantage for black individuals in pursuing careers in technology-related fields. Even after slavery was abolished, racial segregation persisted through Jim Crow laws which further limited opportunities for black people.

Furthermore, discriminatory practices such as redlining and unequal funding for schools perpetuated inequalities. Black neighborhoods were often neglected when it came to infrastructure development and investment in quality education. As a result, many black students did not receive adequate training or exposure to STEM fields during their formative years.

These historical injustices continue to have lasting effects on the representation of black individuals in AI and technology industries today. The lack of diversity within these sectors not only denies talented black individuals' opportunities but also hinders innovation by limiting different perspectives and experiences from contributing to technological advancements.

Lack of Diversity in Hiring Practices: Unveiling the Disparities

An examination of hiring practices reveals significant disparities in diversity within the AI and technology industries. The lack of diversity in these industries is a pressing concern for many individuals who are seeking to belong and be represented. Research indicates that certain racial and ethnic groups, particularly black individuals, are significantly underrepresented in these fields. This underrepresentation can be attributed, at least in part, to hiring practices that perpetuate biases and limit opportunities for diverse candidates.

Studies have shown that unconscious biases play a role in the hiring process, leading to the exclusion of qualified individuals from marginalized communities. These biases may manifest through various mechanisms such as resume screening or interview evaluations. For instance, research has found that resumes with traditionally white-sounding names receive more callbacks compared to those with traditionally black-sounding names, even when qualifications are identical.

Furthermore, there is evidence of networks and connections playing a significant role in recruitment processes within the industry. This creates barriers for those who do not have access to such networks or lack representation within them. As a result, talented individuals from underrepresented backgrounds may face challenges in securing employment opportunities.

Addressing these disparities requires proactive efforts from organizations within the AI and technology industries to implement inclusive hiring practices. Strategies such as blind resume reviews or targeted outreach programs can help mitigate bias and increase diversity among hires. Additionally, fostering an environment that values diversity and promotes belonging can enhance recruitment efforts by attracting diverse talent.

Educational Barriers: Addressing the Gap in Access and Support

Addressing the gap in access and support requires implementing strategies to overcome educational barriers within the industry. The underrepresentation of black individuals in AI and technology industries is influenced by various factors, including limited access to quality education and lack of adequate support systems. To bridge this gap, it is crucial to implement measures that promote equal educational opportunities for all individuals, regardless of their background.

One strategy involves providing scholarships or financial aid programs specifically targeted at black students pursuing degrees in AI and technology-related fields. This would not only alleviate the financial burden but also encourage more black individuals to pursue careers in these industries.

Additionally, creating mentorship programs that connect black students with professionals already working in the field can provide valuable guidance and support throughout their educational journey.

Furthermore, establishing partnerships between universities and industry organizations can help create internship or apprenticeship opportunities for black students. These hands-on experiences are essential for gaining practical skills and exposure to real-world projects, which can subsequently enhance employability prospects.

Moreover, promoting diversity within academic institutions through inclusive policies and outreach initiatives can foster a sense of belonging for black students. This includes ensuring diverse representation among faculty members, offering cultural competency training for staff, and organizing events that celebrate diversity.

Stereotypes and Bias: Challenging Preconceived Notions

Challenging preconceived notions involves critically examining stereotypes and biases that may hinder diversity and inclusion efforts in the AI and technology fields. Stereotypes are generalized beliefs or assumptions about certain groups of people, while biases refer to the tendency to favor one group over another.

In the context of underrepresentation of Black individuals in AI and technology industries, these stereotypes and biases can perpetuate systemic barriers that limit opportunities for diverse talent.

One prevalent stereotype is the assumption that Black individuals lack technical skills or aptitude, which undermines their potential contributions in these fields. This stereotype not only discourages Black individuals from pursuing careers in AI and technology but also contributes to a lack of representation at all levels within organizations. Moreover, unconscious biases can lead to discriminatory practices during recruitment processes, resulting in fewer opportunities for qualified Black candidates.

To challenge these preconceived notions, it is crucial to foster an inclusive environment where diversity is valued and celebrated. This can be achieved through promoting awareness about the harmful effects of stereotypes and biases, implementing bias-mitigating strategies during hiring processes, providing equal access to educational resources and professional development opportunities, as well as actively supporting mentorship programs for underrepresented groups.

Mentorship and Role Models: Nurturing Black Talent in AI and Tech

Mentorship and role models play a vital role in cultivating and nurturing talent within the field of AI and technology. In the context of underrepresentation of black individuals in these industries, mentorship programs can provide valuable guidance, support, and opportunities for aspiring black professionals. By connecting them with experienced mentors who have successfully navigated the challenges of AI and tech careers, these programs can help foster a sense of belonging and empowerment among black individuals.

Effective mentorship involves providing advice on career development, technical skills, networking opportunities, and navigating workplace dynamics. Mentors can also offer insights into overcoming systemic barriers that may disproportionately affect black individuals in these fields. Additionally, having role models who share similar backgrounds and experiences can be highly impactful for aspiring black professionals. Seeing successful individuals who look like them not only provides inspiration but also demonstrates that achieving success is possible.

Moreover, mentorship programs that specifically target underrepresented groups can create a supportive community where participants feel valued and understood. This sense of belonging encourages engagement, retention, and professional growth. It is important to note that mentorship alone cannot fully address the issue of underrepresentation; systemic changes within organizations are necessary to promote diversity and inclusion more broadly.

Nevertheless, mentorship programs serve as an integral component in nurturing black talent within AI and technology industries by providing guidance, support networks, and inspiring role models to foster a sense of belonging among aspiring professionals from underrepresented backgrounds.

Solutions and Best Practices: Promoting Inclusion and Equity

Promoting inclusion and equity in the field of AI and technology requires implementing comprehensive strategies that focus on diversity, representation, and creating inclusive environments. These strategies aim to address the underrepresentation of Black individuals in these industries and foster a sense of belonging for all.

One important step is to increase diversity by actively recruiting and retaining Black talent through targeted outreach programs. This can involve partnering with educational institutions or organizations that support underrepresented communities to identify promising candidates and provide them with access to training opportunities.

Representation is another key aspect of promoting inclusion. It is essential to ensure that diverse voices are heard at all levels within AI and technology organizations. This can be achieved by establishing diverse hiring panels, implementing blind resume screening processes, and promoting unconscious bias training among employees.

Creating inclusive environments is crucial for fostering a sense of belonging among Black individuals in AI and technology fields. Employers should prioritize creating safe spaces where everyone feels comfortable expressing their ideas and perspectives without fear of discrimination or exclusion. Implementing policies against workplace harassment, forming employee resource groups, and providing mentorship opportunities are effective ways to create an inclusive environment.

Frequently Asked Questions

What Are the Specific Historical Events or Policies That Have Contributed to the Underrepresentation of Black Individuals in the AI and Technology Industries?

Historical events and policies have contributed to the underrepresentation of black individuals in AI and technology industries. Identifying these specific factors is crucial for understanding the root causes and developing strategies to promote diversity and inclusion in these fields.

How Do Unconscious Biases and Stereotypes Affect the Hiring Process in the AI and Technology Industries?

Unconscious biases and stereotypes influence the hiring process in AI and technology industries. These biases can lead to the underrepresentation of black individuals, affecting their opportunities for employment and advancement within these fields.

What Are Some Specific Educational Barriers That Black Individuals Face When Pursuing Careers in AI and Technology?

Specific educational barriers faced by black individuals in AI and technology include limited access to quality education, lack of representation and role models, implicit bias in academic settings, inadequate resources and support systems, and racial discrimination affecting opportunities for advancement.

How Can the AI and Technology Industries Challenge and Overcome Preconceived Notions and Biases About the Capabilities and Potential of Black Individuals?

The AI and technology industries can challenge and overcome preconceived notions and biases about the capabilities and potential of black individuals through intentional efforts to diversify their workforce, implement inclusive policies, provide equal opportunities for advancement, and promote cultural competence.

What Are Some Successful Mentorship and Role Model Programs That Have Been Implemented to Support Black Talent in AI and Tech, and What Impact Have They Had?

Successful mentorship and role model programs have been implemented to support black talent in AI and tech. These initiatives aim to provide guidance, opportunities, and representation for black individuals, addressing the underrepresentation issue and promoting diversity in these industries.

Conclusion

In conclusion, the underrepresentation of black individuals in AI and technology industries is a deeply rooted issue that demands immediate attention. The historical context reveals a long-standing lack of diversity, while disparities in hiring practices perpetuate the problem.

Educational barriers further hinder access and support for black talent, while stereotypes and bias create additional challenges. However, by fostering mentorship and providing role models, we can nurture black talent in these fields.

It is crucial to promote inclusion and equity through solutions such as diverse hiring practices and creating an inclusive work environment. Only then can we paint a vibrant picture where every individual, regardless of their background, has equal opportunities to thrive and contribute to the advancements in AI and technology.

The Historical Factors Contributing to This Tech Gap and Their Modern-Day Implications of the Underrepresentation of Black Individuals in AI

Why is there a significant underrepresentation of black individuals in the field of artificial intelligence (AI)? This section aims to explore the historical factors that have contributed to this tech gap and examine their modern-day implications.

By delving into the legacy of slavery and systemic racism, discrimination and bias in data collection and algorithm development, limited access to education and opportunities in STEM fields, as well as the lack of representation and inclusion in AI development and research, we can gain a deeper understanding of the challenges faced by black individuals in AI.

Key Takeaways

- Slavery and systemic racism have hindered black individuals' access to technological advancement opportunities, resulting in a lack of skills necessary for AI careers.
- Discriminatory hiring practices and biased algorithms contribute to the exclusion of black individuals from AI positions.
- Limited access to education and opportunities in STEM fields presents challenges for achieving diversity and inclusivity in technology-related professions.
- The lack of representation and inclusion in AI development and research results in biased algorithms and hinders the development of solutions that address the specific needs of diverse communities.

The Legacy of Slavery and Systemic Racism in Technological Advancement

The underrepresentation of black individuals in AI can be attributed, in part, to the legacy of slavery and systemic racism which have historically hindered their access to technological advancement opportunities. Slavery created a deep racial divide that continues to affect society today. During slavery, African Americans were denied education and subjected to harsh working conditions, limiting their exposure to scientific and technological developments. Even after the abolition of slavery, systemic racism persisted through discriminatory laws and practices such as segregation and unequal access to resources.

These historical factors have had lasting effects on black communities' ability to participate in the tech industry. Limited access to quality education has resulted in a lack of skills necessary for careers in AI development. Additionally, discriminatory hiring practices and biased algorithms contribute to the exclusion of black individuals from AI positions.

Furthermore, the consequences of this underrepresentation extend beyond individual opportunities. The absence of diverse perspectives within AI development perpetuates biases and discrimination in algorithms, leading to skewed outcomes and reinforcing existing inequalities.

Addressing this issue requires acknowledging the historical context that has shaped current disparities. Efforts should focus on creating inclusive educational opportunities for black individuals, combating bias within AI systems, promoting diversity in tech companies, and dismantling systemic barriers that hinder equitable participation in technology fields.

Discrimination and Bias in Data Collection and Algorithm Development

Discrimination and bias can emerge in data collection and algorithm development processes.

These issues are of great concern as they have the potential to perpetuate inequalities and reinforce existing biases in society. To better understand the implications, consider the following:

1. Data Collection Biases: Data used to train algorithms often reflects societal biases, including racial and gender biases. This can result from historical disparities, such as underrepresentation of certain groups or overrepresentation of others in various datasets. Consequently, algorithms may generate biased results that discriminate against marginalized communities.

2. Algorithmic Bias: Algorithms themselves can embed bias if not appropriately designed and tested for fairness. Biased outcomes may occur when algorithms disproportionately favor certain groups or perpetuate discriminatory practices present in historical data sources.

3. Reinforcing Inequities: Discriminatory data collection practices and biased algorithms can further marginalize already disadvantaged individuals or groups. For instance, biased algorithms used in employment screening could disproportionately exclude minority applicants from job opportunities, exacerbating social inequality.

Addressing discrimination and bias in data collection and algorithm development is crucial for creating more inclusive systems that promote belonging for all individuals regardless of their background or identity. It requires active efforts to identify and rectify biases at every stage of the process while promoting diversity within technology development teams to prevent blind spots and foster a more equitable technological landscape.

Limited Access to Education and Opportunities in STEM Fields

Limited access to education and opportunities in STEM fields presents significant challenges for achieving diversity and inclusivity in technology-related professions. The underrepresentation of certain groups, such as black individuals, in these fields can be attributed to various historical factors that have perpetuated systemic inequalities.

Historically, marginalized communities have faced barriers to accessing quality education due to discriminatory policies and practices. This has resulted in limited exposure and opportunities for individuals from these communities to pursue careers in STEM.

Modern-day implications of this limited access include a lack of diverse perspectives within the technology industry. Without representation from various backgrounds, there is a risk of creating technologies that perpetuate biases or fail to address the needs of different communities. Furthermore, the absence of diverse voices can hinder innovation and creativity within the field.

To address this issue, it is essential to provide equitable educational opportunities starting at an early age. Increasing access to quality STEM education for marginalized communities can help bridge the gap and create a more inclusive tech industry. Additionally, fostering mentorship programs and partnerships with organizations focused on diversity and inclusion can support underrepresented individuals in pursuing careers in technology.

Lack of Representation and Inclusion in AI Development and Research

Insufficient representation and inclusivity in the development and research of AI is a pressing concern that hinders the potential for equitable technological advancements. The underrepresentation of certain groups, particularly black individuals, in AI development and research has deep historical roots with far-reaching consequences in today's society.

To understand the magnitude of this issue, it is important to consider:

1. **Exclusionary practices**: Historically, black individuals have been marginalized and excluded from opportunities in STEM fields, including AI research and development. This exclusionary practice has limited their participation and contributions to technological advancements.
2. **Bias in data**: The lack of diversity among those involved in AI research can result in biased algorithms due to the limited perspectives represented during the development process. This bias can perpetuate societal inequalities by reinforcing existing stereotypes or discrimination against marginalized communities.
3. **Ethical implications**: The absence of diverse voices at all stages of AI development raises ethical concerns as decisions made without adequate representation may lead to unintended consequences or reinforce systemic biases.

Addressing these issues requires a concerted effort to increase representation and create inclusive environments within the field of AI development and research. By doing so, we can foster technological advancements that are more equitable, unbiased, and beneficial for all members of society who desire belonging.

Socioeconomic Factors and the Digital Divide: Implications for Black Individuals in AI

Socioeconomic disparities and unequal access to digital resources have created challenges for equitable participation of certain communities in the field of AI. This is particularly evident among black individuals, who face a range of historical and contemporary factors that contribute to underrepresentation in AI. The digital divide, characterized by limited access to technology and internet connectivity, has perpetuated socioeconomic inequalities that hinder black individuals from fully participating in the AI ecosystem.

Historically, discriminatory policies such as redlining and segregation have concentrated poverty within black communities, limiting their access to quality education and resources. These systemic disadvantages continue to affect educational attainment and economic opportunities for black individuals today. As AI becomes increasingly prevalent across various sectors, including finance, healthcare, and criminal justice systems, the lack of representation from diverse backgrounds hampers the development of fair algorithms that can adequately address social issues.

Furthermore, financial barriers associated with pursuing higher education or acquiring technical skills create additional challenges for aspiring black professionals in AI. Limited access to computer science programs or coding boot camps further exacerbates the underrepresentation problem.

Addressing these disparities requires concerted efforts by policymakers, educators, and industry leaders to increase accessibility and promote inclusivity in AI development. Initiatives such as scholarships targeting underrepresented groups can help alleviate financial burdens while mentorship programs foster a supportive environment for aspiring black individuals interested in pursuing careers in AI.

Frequently Asked Questions

What Are the Specific Historical Events That Have Contributed to

the Underrepresentation of Black Individuals in AI?

Specific historical events, such as systemic racism, limited access to education and resources, discriminatory hiring practices, and biased algorithms have contributed to the underrepresentation of black individuals in AI. These factors continue to perpetuate inequalities in the field.

How Has Discrimination and Bias in Data Collection and Algorithm Development Affected the Representation of Black Individuals in AI?

Discrimination and bias in data collection and algorithm development have adversely affected the representation of black individuals in AI. These factors have perpetuated a tech gap, resulting in underrepresentation and limited opportunities for black individuals in the field of AI.

What Are Some Examples of Limited Access to Education and Opportunities in STEM Fields for Black Individuals, and How Has This Impacted Their Representation in AI?

Limited access to education and opportunities in STEM fields for black individuals has adversely affected their representation in AI. This lack of inclusion can be likened to a puzzle missing critical pieces, hindering the development of comprehensive and diverse AI systems.

How Does the Lack of Representation and Inclusion in AI Development and Research Affect the Advancement and Innovation of AI Technologies?

The lack of representation and inclusion in AI development and research has implications for the advancement and innovation of AI technologies. It can limit diverse perspectives, perpetuate biases, and hinder the creation of fair and equitable AI systems.

What Are the Socioeconomic Factors That Contribute to the Digital Divide and Its Implications for Black Individuals in AI?

The socioeconomic factors contributing to the digital divide and their implications for black individuals in AI are multifaceted. These factors include limited access to education, lack of representation, systemic discrimination, and unequal distribution of resources which perpetuate disparities in AI participation and opportunities.

Conclusion

In conclusion, the historical factors contributing to the tech gap and the underrepresentation of black individuals in AI are deeply intertwined with systemic racism and discrimination.

The legacy of slavery has perpetuated inequalities and limited access to education and opportunities in STEM fields. Discrimination and bias in data collection and algorithm development further exacerbate this issue.

Moreover, the lack of representation and inclusion in AI development hinders progress towards equity. Socioeconomic factors, such as the digital divide, compound these challenges.

Addressing these complex issues is crucial for achieving a more inclusive and equitable future in AI.

The Importance of Diversity in AI Development and Decision-Making

The pursuit of diversity in AI development and decision-making has emerged as a critical concern in contemporary society. As technological advancements continue to shape various aspects of our lives, it is paramount to acknowledge the multifaceted implications of this issue.

This section aims to explore the role of diversity in AI development, identify challenges in promoting diversity in AI decision-making processes, examine the benefits of including diverse perspectives in AI design, analyze ethical implications arising from a lack of diversity, and propose strategies for increasing inclusivity within these realms.

Key Takeaways

- Incorporating diverse perspectives and experiences is crucial for fair and unbiased decision-making processes in AI development.
- Unintentional biases can be embedded within algorithms due to limited representation or understanding of certain groups' needs and experiences.
- Diverse perspectives lead to more robust and inclusive outcomes in AI systems.
- Lack of diversity in AI development can result in ethical implications that perpetuate discrimination and reinforce inequalities.

The Role of Diversity in AI Development

The role of diversity in AI development encompasses the recognition that incorporating diverse perspectives and experiences is crucial for ensuring fair and unbiased decision-making processes. Diversity in AI development refers to the inclusion of individuals from various backgrounds, such as different races, genders, ethnicities, cultures, and socioeconomic statuses. By incorporating diverse perspectives into AI development, it becomes possible to address the limitations and biases that may arise from a homogeneous group.

Including diverse voices in AI development helps to mitigate the risk of perpetuating unfair biases or discriminatory practices. Unintentional biases can be embedded within algorithms due to limited representation or understanding of certain groups' needs and experiences. This can result in biased decisions or outcomes that disproportionately affect specific communities.

Furthermore, diversity brings together a wide range of expertise and knowledge that can enhance problem-solving abilities. Different perspectives offer unique insights and approaches to addressing complex challenges related to AI development. By embracing diversity, AI systems can be designed more inclusively and responsibly.

Challenges in Promoting Diversity in AI Decision-Making

Challenges arise in fostering a diverse range of perspectives and experiences within the decision-making processes of artificial intelligence. While diversity is widely recognized as crucial for the development and deployment of AI systems, achieving it remains a complex task.

One challenge lies in addressing biases embedded in AI algorithms, which can perpetuate discrimination and exclusion. These biases often result from limited datasets that fail to capture the full spectrum of human experiences. Additionally, there is a lack of diversity among AI researchers, developers, and data scientists themselves. This homogeneity can lead to blind spots and reinforce existing biases within the technology.

Another challenge is ensuring equitable access to resources and opportunities in AI development.

Historically marginalized groups face barriers such as limited access to education, funding, or technological infrastructure, making it difficult for them to participate fully in shaping AI decision-making processes.

Furthermore, ethical considerations play a significant role in promoting diversity within AI decision-making. The potential social impact of biased algorithms or discriminatory outcomes underscores the importance of incorporating diverse perspectives early on in system design.

To address these challenges effectively, collaborative efforts involving diverse stakeholders are necessary. Engaging with individuals from various backgrounds can help identify hidden biases, mitigate risks associated with exclusionary practices, and foster inclusivity throughout the entire lifecycle of AI technologies.

Benefits of Including Diverse Perspectives in AI Design

Including diverse perspectives in the design of artificial intelligence systems can lead to more robust and inclusive outcomes. The inclusion of diverse perspectives is crucial as it brings together a range of experiences, knowledge, and values that can help overcome biases and limitations inherent in AI development. By incorporating input from individuals with different backgrounds, cultures, genders, races, and abilities, AI systems can be designed to better understand and address the needs of diverse populations.

Diverse perspectives also contribute to the ethical development of AI systems. Ethical considerations are essential in ensuring that these technologies do not perpetuate discrimination or reinforce existing inequalities. Including individuals from underrepresented groups in the decision-making process helps identify potential biases early on and promotes fairness and accountability.

Moreover, diversity fosters innovation by encouraging creativity and out-of-the-box thinking. Different viewpoints challenge established norms and assumptions, leading to novel solutions that benefit society at large. In addition, when people feel represented and included in the development process, they are more likely to trust AI systems and engage with them.

Ethical Implications of Lacking Diversity in AI Development

Lacking diversity in AI development can result in ethical implications that perpetuate discrimination and reinforce existing inequalities. The development of artificial intelligence (AI) systems is driven by human decisions, biases, and values. If the individuals involved in AI design and decision-making processes come from similar backgrounds or possess homogeneous perspectives, there is a risk of introducing biased algorithms that may discriminate against certain groups.

One ethical implication of lacking diversity in AI development is the potential for algorithmic bias. When training data primarily represents certain demographics or excludes others, AI systems can inadvertently learn and perpetuate discriminatory patterns. This can lead to biased outcomes in areas such as hiring practices, criminal justice, or access to financial resources, further marginalizing already disadvantaged communities.

Moreover, without diverse representation at the table during AI development, considerations of different cultural norms, values, and experiences may be overlooked. This lack of diversity can hinder the ability of AI systems to adequately address the needs and preferences of all users.

To mitigate these ethical implications and ensure fairness and inclusivity within AI technologies, it is crucial to prioritize diversity in both the workforce developing these systems and the datasets used for training them. By incorporating a variety of perspectives into AI design processes, we can help create more equitable algorithms that benefit a broader range of individuals while minimizing potential harm caused by biased decision-making.

Strategies for Increasing Diversity in AI Development and Decision-Making

One effective strategy for promoting a more inclusive and representative environment in AI development involves fostering collaboration among individuals from diverse backgrounds and perspectives. This approach recognizes the importance of embracing diversity not only for ethical reasons but also to enhance the quality and fairness of AI systems.

By encouraging collaboration among individuals with different experiences, knowledge, and cultural perspectives, we can ensure that AI technologies are developed in a manner that considers the needs and values of diverse communities. This collaborative process allows for a broader range of ideas, insights, and approaches to be considered during AI development, leading to more robust solutions that address a wider array of societal challenges.

Moreover, fostering collaboration among diverse individuals helps to mitigate biases present in current AI systems. By bringing together individuals who possess different social identities, professional backgrounds, and lived experiences, it becomes possible to identify and rectify biased assumptions or discriminatory outcomes that may arise from existing algorithms.

Frequently Asked Questions

How Does Diversity in AI Development Contribute to Better Decision-Making?

Diversity in AI development contributes to better decision-making by bringing in different perspectives, experiences, and knowledge. This enhances problem-solving abilities, reduces biases, improves fairness, and ensures that the technology caters to the needs of a wide range of users.

What Are Some Specific Challenges Faced in Promoting Diversity in AI Decision-Making?

Challenges in promoting diversity in AI decision-making include the underrepresentation of certain groups, biases embedded in algorithms, and lack of diverse perspectives. These obstacles hinder equitable and inclusive outcomes, reinforcing existing power dynamics.

Can Including Diverse Perspectives in AI Design Lead to More Accurate and Fair Outcomes?

Including diverse perspectives in AI design can lead to more accurate and fair outcomes. By incorporating a range of viewpoints, biases and limitations of the technology can be identified and mitigated, resulting in improved performance and equitable decision-making.

What Are the Potential Ethical Implications of Lacking Diversity in AI Development?

The potential ethical implications of lacking diversity in AI development include the reinforcement of biased algorithms, discriminatory decision-making processes, and perpetuation of social inequalities. This can be likened to a distorted mirror reflecting and amplifying existing biases and prejudices.

What Strategies Can Be Implemented to Increase Diversity in AI Development and Decision-Making?

Strategies to increase diversity in AI development and decision-making include promoting inclusive hiring practices, providing equal opportunities for underrepresented groups, creating diverse teams, and implementing diversity training programs.

Conclusion

In conclusion, diversity plays a crucial role in AI development and decision-making. The challenges in promoting diversity must be acknowledged, but the benefits of including diverse perspectives are undeniable.

Lacking diversity can lead to ethical implications that can harm society as a whole. Therefore, strategies for increasing diversity in AI development and decision-making should be implemented to ensure fairness and inclusivity.

By embracing diversity, we can create AI systems that truly reflect the needs and values of all individuals, evoking a sense of unity and empowerment among the audience.

How Early AI Education for Black Children Can Contribute to Closing This Tech Gap

In today's increasingly technology-driven society, the need to bridge the tech gap among different communities has become a pressing concern.

This section explores the potential of early AI education for black children in contributing to the closure of this gap. By examining the importance of such education and its impact on promoting diversity and inclusion, as well as discussing strategies for implementation and long-term effects on tech skills, we aim to shed light on this significant issue and provide insights for fostering belonging and equity in technological advancement.

Key Takeaways

- Early AI education for black children can provide equal opportunities in the tech industry.
- It equips them with essential skills for future careers in AI and technology.
- AI education fosters critical thinking and problem-solving abilities.
- It empowers black children to become innovators and creators.

The Importance of Early AI Education for Black Children

The importance of early AI education for black children lies in its potential to contribute to closing the tech gap. By providing opportunities for young black students to learn about artificial intelligence (AI) at an early age, we can empower them with the skills and knowledge necessary to thrive in a technology-driven society. Access to AI education can help bridge the digital divide that disproportionately affects marginalized communities.

Early exposure to AI education allows black children to develop a strong foundation in computational thinking, problem-solving, and critical analysis. These skills are essential for success in a rapidly evolving technological landscape. By introducing AI concepts early on, we can nurture their interest and curiosity, fostering a sense of belonging and encouraging them to pursue careers in STEM fields.

Furthermore, incorporating diversity into AI education is crucial for creating inclusive technologies. Black children bring unique perspectives and experiences that can influence the development of more equitable algorithms and systems. By involving diverse voices from an early stage, we can avoid biased outcomes that perpetuate existing inequalities.

Addressing the Tech Gap through AI Education Initiatives

Addressing the tech gap through initiatives focused on educating marginalized communities about artificial intelligence can help bridge the divide and promote equitable access to technology. By providing early AI education for black children, we can empower them with the knowledge and skills necessary to thrive in a technology-driven world.

These initiatives have the potential to foster a sense of belonging and empowerment within marginalized communities by:

- Enhancing opportunities: AI education equips individuals with valuable skills that are increasingly in demand across industries. By providing access to this education, marginalized communities can gain equal footing in the job market, opening up new avenues for economic growth and social mobility.

- Fostering innovation: By empowering black children with AI education, we tap into diverse perspectives and experiences, which can drive innovation. This not only benefits these individuals but also society as a whole by nurturing inclusive technological advancements.
- Building confidence: Early exposure to AI education instills confidence in black children, showing them that they have the ability to understand and contribute to cutting-edge technologies. This self-assurance helps cultivate a sense of belonging within technology-related fields.
- Promoting representation: Educating marginalized communities about AI ensures that they are not left behind in an increasingly digital world. It encourages diversity and inclusivity within the field of artificial intelligence, ultimately leading to more equitable outcomes for all individuals involved.

Promoting Diversity and Inclusion in AI Education for Black Children

Promoting diversity and inclusion in AI education for black children necessitates creating opportunities for marginalized communities to engage with cutting-edge technologies. By providing access to AI education, we can contribute to closing the tech gap that currently exists between different racial groups.

Research has shown that early exposure to AI concepts and tools can enhance critical thinking skills, problem-solving abilities, and computational thinking among students. This is particularly important for black children who have historically been underrepresented in the field of technology.

Engaging black children in AI education not only helps bridge the tech gap but also promotes social equity. By empowering these communities with knowledge and skills related to AI, we enable them to participate actively in the digital economy and shape future technological developments. Moreover, fostering diversity within the AI field is essential for creating inclusive solutions that address a wide range of societal needs.

To promote belongingness in this context, it is crucial to design AI education initiatives that are culturally responsive and sensitive to the experiences of black children. This involves incorporating diverse perspectives into curriculum development, ensuring representation of black role models in STEM fields, and establishing mentorship programs that provide support and guidance throughout their educational journey.

Closing the Tech Gap: Strategies for Implementing Early AI Education

Implementing early AI education strategies can play a crucial role in bridging the disparities in technological knowledge among different communities. By providing black children with access to AI education from an early age, we can empower them to navigate and excel in the rapidly evolving digital landscape. This not only helps to address the technology gap but also contributes to fostering diversity and inclusion within the field of artificial intelligence.

Increased opportunities: Early AI education equips black children with the necessary skills and knowledge to actively participate in emerging tech industries, opening doors for better career prospects and economic empowerment.

Empowerment and agency: Early exposure to AI education empowers black children by instilling confidence, self-belief, and a sense of belonging within a field that has historically been dominated by certain demographics.

Overcoming biases: By introducing AI education at an early stage, we can challenge racial biases present in technology development processes, ensuring that future innovations are inclusive and representative of diverse perspectives.

Cultivating innovation: Early AI education fosters creativity, critical thinking, problem-solving skills, and collaboration among black children. This cultivates an environment where innovative ideas from diverse backgrounds can thrive.

The Long-Term Impact of Early AI Education on Black Children's Tech Skills

The long-term impact of early exposure to AI education on the technological skills of black children remains a topic of interest within the field. Research suggests that providing AI education at an early age can have significant positive effects on the development of these skills. By introducing black children to AI concepts and tools, they are given the opportunity to engage with technology in a meaningful way and gain valuable knowledge and skills that can contribute to closing the tech gap.

Early exposure to AI education equips black children with foundational knowledge in areas such as coding, problem-solving, critical thinking, and data analysis. These skills are essential for success in today's technology-driven world. Moreover, by engaging with AI education at a young age, black children develop familiarity and comfort with emerging technologies, increasing their confidence in using and exploring them further.

Furthermore, early exposure to AI education has been shown to foster a strong interest in technology among black children. This interest can lead them down educational pathways focused on fields like computer science or engineering. By encouraging this interest from an early age, we can help cultivate diverse talent pools within these industries and promote greater representation of black individuals in tech-related careers.

Frequently Asked Questions

What Are Some Potential Barriers or Challenges in Implementing Early AI Education for Black Children?

Potential barriers or challenges in implementing early AI education for Black children may include limited access to resources, lack of representation and diverse role models, systemic inequalities in education, and the need for culturally responsive curriculum and pedagogy.

How Can AI Education Initiatives Specifically Target and Address the Needs of Black Children?

Targeted AI education initiatives can address the needs of black children by providing equitable access, culturally relevant content, and inclusive learning environments. These efforts contribute to closing the tech gap by promoting diversity and ensuring equal opportunities for underrepresented groups.

Are There Any Successful Examples of AI Education Programs That Have Already Been Implemented for Black Children?

Successful examples of AI education programs for black children exist. These initiatives have effectively targeted and addressed the specific needs of black students, contributing to closing the tech gap and promoting inclusivity in the field of AI.

What Are Some Specific Strategies or Approaches That Can Be Used

to Close the Tech Gap Through Early AI Education?

Early AI education for Black children can contribute to closing the tech gap by providing equal access and opportunities, fostering interest and confidence in technology, developing relevant skills, promoting diversity in the field, and addressing systemic barriers.

How Does Early AI Education Contribute to the Overall Development and Empowerment of Black Children, Beyond Just Their Tech Skills?

Early AI education for Black children contributes to their overall development and empowerment by cultivating critical thinking, problem-solving, and creativity. It fosters a sense of agency, enhances digital literacy skills, and promotes inclusivity in the technology field, facilitating social mobility and reducing the tech gap.

Conclusion

In conclusion, early AI education for black children holds immense importance in closing the tech gap. By addressing this gap through AI education initiatives and promoting diversity and inclusion, we can ensure equal opportunities for all.

Implementing strategies for early AI education will help develop essential tech skills in black children, creating a long-term impact on their future success.

As the old adage goes, 'Give a man a fish and you feed him for a day; teach a man to fish and you feed him for a lifetime.' Providing early AI education equips black children with the tools they need to thrive in the rapidly advancing technological landscape.

CHAPTER 4: FOSTERING DIGITAL CONFIDENCE

The Concept of Digital Confidence and Its Relevance in the Modern World

In today's technologically advanced society, the concept of digital confidence holds significant relevance. The ability to navigate and utilize digital tools effectively has become a crucial aspect of personal and professional success.

This section seeks to explore the multifaceted nature of digital confidence, delving into its foundations, psychological aspects, and strategies for building it.

By examining the role of digital confidence in various contexts, this section aims to provide insights into its importance in our modern world.

Key Takeaways

- Digital confidence is essential for individuals to effectively navigate and engage with technology, enabling them to participate fully in various aspects of life.
- Building digital confidence requires technical proficiency, understanding of online resources, critical thinking skills, responsible online behavior, and ethical conduct.
- Self-efficacy, social influence, past experiences, and subjective evaluation shape an individual's level of digital confidence and sense of belonging in the online community.
- To build digital confidence, individuals should set goals, seek opportunities for practice, stay updated with technology trends, connect with online communities, and engage in courses or workshops for guidance and support.

The Importance of Digital Confidence in Today's Society

The significance of digital confidence in contemporary society lies in its ability to empower individuals to navigate and engage with technology effectively and securely. In today's increasingly digital world, technology has become an integral part of our daily lives. From online banking to social media platforms, the use of technology has become ubiquitous.

However, with this increased reliance on technology comes the need for individuals to possess a certain level of digital confidence.

Digital confidence refers to an individual's belief in their ability to use and interact with digital technologies. It encompasses knowledge, skills, and attitudes necessary for effective and secure engagement with technology. Having digital confidence allows individuals to make informed decisions about their online activities, protect their personal information from cyber threats, and effectively utilize various technological tools and resources available.

In contemporary society, where almost every aspect of life is influenced by digital technologies, having digital confidence is crucial for full participation in social, economic, educational, and political spheres. Those who lack digital confidence may find themselves at a disadvantage when it comes to accessing opportunities or resources that are predominantly available online.

Moreover, possessing digital confidence contributes to a sense of belonging within the modern society that heavily relies on technology as a means of communication and interaction. By being digitally confident, individuals can actively participate in online communities or discussions without feeling alienated or excluded due to limited technological literacy.

Overall, the importance of digital confidence cannot be overstated in today's society. It not only empowers individuals but also fosters inclusivity by ensuring everyone feels equipped to navigate the ever-evolving landscape of technology confidently and securely.

Understanding the Foundations of Digital Confidence

Foundations of digital confidence can be better comprehended by analyzing individuals' abilities to navigate and utilize technology effectively. In today's interconnected world, possessing the necessary skills to confidently engage with digital technologies is crucial for personal, professional, and social growth. Digital confidence refers to an individual's belief in their own ability to use digital tools and platforms competently and securely.

At its core, digital confidence is built upon a solid foundation of technical proficiency. This includes having a good understanding of basic computer operations, such as using software applications, navigating operating systems, and troubleshooting common issues. Additionally, individuals need to be adept at utilizing online resources effectively for tasks such as information retrieval, communication, and collaboration.

However, digital confidence extends beyond mere technical competence. It also encompasses the development of critical thinking skills to evaluate the reliability and credibility of online information sources. Individuals must be able to discern between accurate information and misinformation in order to make informed decisions.

Moreover, being digitally confident involves practicing responsible online behavior. This includes protecting personal data privacy through secure practices like strong passwords and encryption methods. Furthermore, individuals should cultivate ethical conduct when engaging with others online by respecting diversity of opinions and promoting positive interactions.

Understanding these foundations of digital confidence empowers individuals to navigate the complex digital landscape with ease while fostering a sense of belonging within the wider community that values technological literacy.

Exploring the Psychological Aspects of Digital Confidence

Psychological factors play an instrumental role in shaping individuals' beliefs and attitudes towards their abilities to effectively engage with digital technologies. The concept of digital confidence encompasses an individual's subjective evaluation of their competence and comfort in using digital tools and platforms. It is influenced by several psychological aspects that are integral to an individual's sense of belonging in the modern world.

Self-efficacy, or one's belief in their ability to successfully perform specific tasks, has been identified as a key psychological factor affecting digital confidence. Individuals who possess higher levels of self-efficacy tend to be more confident in their ability to navigate through various technological interfaces and adapt to new digital environments.

Furthermore, social influence plays a significant role in shaping individuals' beliefs about their digital abilities. People often compare themselves with others around them, forming judgments based on perceived norms and standards. Positive feedback from peers or mentors can enhance individuals' self-perception of their digital capabilities and foster a sense of belonging within the online community.

Additionally, past experiences with technology can shape one's level of digital confidence. Positive experiences, such as successful problem-solving or achieving desired outcomes through technology use, can bolster an individual's belief in their own proficiency. Conversely, negative experiences or challenges faced may lead to feelings of incompetence or insecurity when engaging with digital technologies.

Building Digital Confidence: Tips and Strategies

Building digital confidence requires individuals to employ various strategies and techniques aimed at enhancing their competence and comfort in using technology. In today's increasingly digital world, the ability to navigate and utilize technology effectively is crucial for social belonging and participation.

To build digital confidence, individuals can start by setting specific goals for themselves in terms of what they aim to achieve with technology. This could include learning how to use a new software or application or improving one's proficiency with existing tools. Additionally, seeking out opportunities for practice and hands-on experience can significantly contribute to building digital confidence. Engaging in online courses, webinars, or workshops that offer guidance and support can help individuals develop their skills and overcome any hesitations or fears associated with technology use.

Another important aspect of building digital confidence is staying up to date with current trends and advancements in technology. By actively seeking information about emerging technologies, individuals can stay informed about new features or tools that could potentially enhance their abilities or streamline their tasks. Moreover, connecting with like-minded individuals through online communities or forums can provide a sense of belonging and create opportunities for collaboration and knowledge-sharing.

Overcoming Digital Insecurities: A Journey to Digital Confidence

To overcome digital insecurities, individuals can engage in activities that promote familiarity and comfort with technology. This journey towards digital confidence involves various steps that can help individuals navigate the digital landscape with ease and assurance.

Education and Skill Development:
- Taking online courses or attending workshops to enhance technical skills.
- Participating in webinars or conferences to stay updated on the latest technological advancements.

Practice and Exposure:
- Actively using technology in daily life, such as managing personal finances through online banking or shopping online.

- Exploring new software applications or gadgets to broaden knowledge and experience.

By actively participating in these activities, individuals can gradually overcome their digital insecurities and build a sense of belonging in the digital world. Engaging in continuous learning helps individuals gain confidence by acquiring new skills and staying up to date with technological advancements.

Regularly practicing using technology also aids in familiarizing oneself with various platforms, reducing anxiety related to unfamiliar interfaces. Through this journey, one can develop a sense of belonging within the digital community, fostering connections with others who share similar interests and experiences.

The Role of Digital Confidence in Personal and Professional Success

The role of digital confidence in personal and professional success can be understood by examining the impact it has on individuals' ability to navigate the increasingly technology-driven landscape. In today's society, where digital technologies are ubiquitous, possessing digital confidence is crucial for individuals to thrive both personally and professionally.

Digital confidence refers to an individual's belief in their own abilities to effectively use and navigate digital technologies. It encompasses a range of skills, including technical proficiency, information literacy, critical thinking, and online safety awareness. With the rapid advancement of technology, individuals who lack digital confidence may find themselves at a disadvantage in various aspects of their lives.

In personal contexts, having digital confidence allows individuals to connect with others through social media platforms, access online resources for entertainment or learning purposes, and engage in e-commerce activities securely. Moreover, it enables them to participate actively in the global community by sharing ideas and collaborating with people from diverse backgrounds.

In professional settings, digital confidence plays a significant role in career advancement. Employers increasingly expect employees to possess strong digital skills that enable them to adapt quickly to technological changes and utilize digital tools efficiently. Individuals who demonstrate high levels of digital confidence are more likely to excel in their roles and contribute positively towards achieving organizational goals.

Overall, developing digital confidence is essential for both personal fulfillment and professional success in our technology-driven world. It empowers individuals to embrace new opportunities presented by advancements in technology while navigating potential challenges effectively. By fostering a sense of belonging within the ever-expanding virtual community, digital confidence becomes a pathway towards personal growth and achievement.

Frequently Asked Questions

How Does Digital Confidence Impact Our Daily Lives?

Digital confidence impacts daily lives by enabling individuals to navigate and engage with digital technologies effectively. It fosters a sense of empowerment, self-assurance, and competence, allowing individuals to fully participate in the modern world's digital landscape.

Can Lack of Digital Confidence Affect Our Mental Well-Being?

The lack of digital confidence can potentially impact mental well-being. It may lead to feelings of frustration, anxiety, and inadequacy when navigating the digital world. This highlights the importance of developing digital skills and knowledge for overall mental health in the modern era.

What Are Some Common Challenges People Face in Building Digital Confidence?

Common challenges in building digital confidence include fear of technology, lack of knowledge and skills, concerns about privacy and security, difficulties with information overload, and the need to adapt to rapidly evolving digital tools and platforms.

How Can Digital Confidence Contribute to Career Growth and Advancement?

Digital confidence can contribute to career growth and advancement by enabling individuals to effectively navigate digital technologies and platforms, enhancing their productivity, communication, and problem-solving skills, and staying competitive in today's digitally driven job market.

Are There Any Specific Strategies or Techniques to Overcome Digital Insecurities?

To overcome digital insecurities, specific strategies and techniques can be employed. These may include increasing digital literacy, practicing safe online behavior, seeking professional guidance, and engaging in continuous learning to adapt to evolving technologies.

Conclusion

In conclusion, the concept of digital confidence holds great relevance in the modern world. It plays a crucial role in both personal and professional success, as it enables individuals to navigate the digital landscape with ease and proficiency.

By understanding the foundations and psychological aspects of digital confidence, one can build upon it using various tips and strategies. Overcoming digital insecurities is a journey that requires self-reflection and continuous learning.

Embracing digital confidence empowers individuals to harness the full potential of technology, leading to a more fulfilling and successful life.

Concerns About the "Digital Divide" and How Early AI Education Can Mitigate Its Effects

As technology continues to advance, concerns about the 'digital divide' and its impact on education have become increasingly prevalent. According to recent statistics, it is estimated that around 3.6 billion people still lack access to the internet, hindering their ability to participate fully in the digital age.

This section aims to address these concerns by exploring how early AI education can mitigate the effects of the digital divide. By understanding the factors contributing to this divide and implementing effective strategies, we can foster inclusivity and bridge the gap for individuals who are currently excluded from technological advancements.

Key Takeaways

- Disparities in access to technology create a gap in educational opportunities, known as the digital divide.
- AI can play a significant role in bridging the digital divide by enhancing access to technology and internet connectivity.
- Early AI education is a solution to the digital divide as it equips individuals with essential technological skills, promotes inclusivity, and identifies talent in the field.
- Strategies for implementing early AI education programs include involving various stakeholders, providing equal access, fostering collaboration, and emphasizing educator training and professional development.

The Impact of the Digital Divide on Education

The impact of the digital divide on education has been a significant concern, with disparities in access to technology hindering equal opportunities for learning. The digital divide refers to the gap between those who have access to and can effectively use digital technologies and those who do not.

In today's increasingly digital world, access to technology is crucial for students to acquire the necessary skills and knowledge for future success. However, not all students have equal access to technology due to factors such as socioeconomic status, geographic location, and infrastructure limitations.

This lack of access creates a disparity in educational opportunities among students. Those without access to technology are at a disadvantage when it comes to accessing online resources, participating in virtual classrooms, and developing digital literacy skills. As a result, they may struggle to keep up with their digitally literate peers and miss out on important learning opportunities.

Furthermore, the impact of the digital divide extends beyond academic achievement. Access to technology also plays a vital role in preparing students for the workforce. In today's job market, digital skills are highly valued by employers across various industries. Without adequate exposure and training in using digital tools and platforms, students from disadvantaged backgrounds may face difficulties competing for jobs or pursuing higher education.

Addressing the digital divide is crucial for ensuring equitable educational opportunities for all students. Efforts should be made at multiple levels – from policymakers implementing initiatives that promote accessibility and affordability of technology in underserved communities, to educators integrating technology into their instructional practices and offering support for students without home internet access.

Understanding the Factors Contributing to the Digital Divide

Understanding the factors contributing to disparities in access to technology and internet connectivity is crucial in bridging the digital divide. Various factors contribute to this divide, including socioeconomic status, geographic location, age, race/ethnicity, and educational attainment.

Socioeconomic status plays a significant role as individuals with lower incomes may not have the financial means to afford internet service or purchase devices necessary for accessing technology.

Geographic location also affects access as rural areas often lack reliable internet infrastructure compared to urban areas.

Age can be another factor as older adults may face challenges in adopting and using technology.

Additionally, racial and ethnic minorities may experience disparities due to systemic inequalities that limit their access to resources.

Lastly, educational attainment can impact individuals' ability to access technology, as those with lower education levels may have less exposure and familiarity with digital tools.

Understanding these factors enables policymakers and stakeholders to develop targeted interventions such as providing affordable internet options, improving infrastructure in underserved areas, offering digital literacy programs for older adults, addressing systemic inequalities through policy changes, and integrating technology education into school curricula.

Exploring the Role of AI in Bridging the Digital Divide

Exploring the role of AI in bridging the digital divide necessitates an examination of its potential to enhance access to technology and internet connectivity across various socioeconomic, geographic, and demographic groups.

AI can play a significant role in increasing access by providing innovative solutions to overcome barriers such as affordability, infrastructure limitations, and lack of digital literacy.

One way AI can bridge the digital divide is through the development of low-cost devices that are affordable for individuals from lower socioeconomic backgrounds. These devices can be equipped with AI-driven features that optimize performance and reduce costs without compromising functionality.

Additionally, AI algorithms can be utilized to improve internet connectivity in remote areas by optimizing signal strength and coverage.

Another area where AI can contribute is in addressing the issue of digital literacy. Through intelligent tutoring systems powered by AI, individuals can receive personalized learning experiences tailored to their specific needs and skill levels. This not only enhances their understanding of technology but also equips them with essential digital skills necessary for full participation in today's digitally driven society.

Furthermore, AI-powered chatbots and virtual assistants offer opportunities for individuals with limited access or familiarity with technology to engage with online platforms more easily. These tools provide guidance and support, answering questions and assisting users in navigating various digital platforms.

Early AI Education: A Solution to Addressing the Digital Divide

One potential solution in bridging the digital divide is to incorporate AI education at an early stage, which can aid in equipping individuals with essential technological skills. In today's increasingly digitized world, having a solid foundation in AI education can provide individuals with the necessary tools to navigate and thrive in a technology-driven society. By introducing AI concepts at an early age, students can develop critical thinking skills, problem-solving abilities, and computational thinking that are essential for understanding and utilizing AI technologies effectively.

Early AI education also has the potential to promote inclusivity and belonging among individuals who may otherwise be left behind due to the digital divide. By providing equal access to AI education opportunities from an early stage, regardless of socio-economic status or geographic location, we can ensure that all individuals have a fair chance at acquiring essential technological skills. This not only empowers individuals but also contributes to creating a more inclusive and equitable society.

Furthermore, incorporating AI education at an early stage allows for the identification and nurturing of talent in this field. By exposing young minds to AI concepts and applications, we can inspire interest and passion for this rapidly evolving field. This not only helps bridge the digital divide but also cultivates a diverse pool of future professionals who can contribute to advancements in artificial intelligence.

Strategies for Implementing Early AI Education Programs

Implementing effective strategies for early AI education programs requires careful planning, coordination, and collaboration among various stakeholders in the educational system. To ensure the successful implementation of these programs, it is essential to involve teachers, school administrators, policymakers, parents, and industry experts.

Firstly, clear learning objectives need to be established to guide the curriculum design and instructional practices. These objectives should align with national or international standards in order to provide students with a solid foundation in AI concepts and skills. Additionally, educators should have access to training and professional development opportunities that equip them with the necessary knowledge and pedagogical strategies to effectively teach AI concepts.

Collaboration between schools and industry partners is crucial for providing real-world applications of AI education. Industry experts can contribute their expertise by offering mentorship programs or facilitating internships that expose students to practical applications of AI technology. This collaboration also helps ensure that the curriculum remains up to date with current trends and developments in the field.

Furthermore, establishing partnerships with relevant organizations can help secure funding for resources such as hardware, software licenses, and training materials. These partnerships can also provide networking opportunities for educators and allow them to share best practices.

Frequently Asked Questions

What Are Some Specific Examples of How the Digital Divide Affects Education?

The digital divide in education is evidenced through limited access to online resources and educational platforms, hindering students' ability to obtain necessary information and engage in virtual learning environments.

How Does Socioeconomic Status Contribute to the Digital Divide?

Socioeconomic status contributes to the digital divide by influencing access to technology and internet connectivity. Individuals with lower socioeconomic status are more likely to lack resources, such as computers and high-speed internet, limiting their ability to participate fully in the digital world.

Can AI Technology Alone Bridge the Digital Divide?

AI technology alone cannot bridge the digital divide. While it can enhance access to information and services, socioeconomic factors such as income and education play a significant role in determining individuals' ability to benefit from AI advancements.

Are There Any Challenges or Limitations to Implementing Early AI Education Programs?

Challenges and limitations to implementing early AI education programs include lack of resources, inadequate teacher training, and the potential for exacerbating existing inequities. These factors may hinder effective implementation and limit the impact of such initiatives.

What Are Some Successful Strategies That Have Been Used to Implement Early AI Education Programs?

Successful strategies for implementing early AI education programs include curriculum integration, teacher training, and partnerships with industry experts. These approaches have been effective in equipping students with necessary skills and preparing them for future technological advancements.

Conclusion

In conclusion, the digital divide poses significant challenges to education, limiting access and opportunities for many. However, through the implementation of early AI education programs, we can bridge this gap and empower individuals with essential digital skills.

By equipping students with knowledge of AI technologies from an early age, we lay a strong foundation for their future success in an increasingly digitized world.

Just as a beacon of light illuminates even the darkest corners, early AI education shines a path towards a more inclusive and equitable future.

Stories of Black Children Gaining Confidence through AI Projects

According to recent data, black children often face unique challenges that can impact their confidence and self-esteem.

However, the emergence of artificial intelligence (AI) projects has provided a platform for empowering these children and fostering their sense of worth.

This section aims to share stories of how AI projects have inspired black children to explore this field, ultimately boosting their confidence and instilling a belief in their own abilities.

By highlighting these narratives of resilience and achievement, we hope to celebrate black excellence in AI while igniting a desire for belonging in our audience.

Key Takeaways

- AI projects for black children provide personalized learning experiences and promote improved academic performance and enhanced self-esteem.
- Engaging with AI projects fosters a sense of empowerment and belonging within the field, allowing black children to challenge themselves intellectually and develop critical thinking skills.
- AI initiatives create a supportive environment where black children feel valued, accepted, and part of a collaborative community.
- Participation in AI projects helps black children overcome challenges, boosts their self-esteem, and empowers them to pursue further opportunities in the field.

The Power of AI in Empowering Black Children

The power of artificial intelligence (AI) in empowering black children is evidenced by the stories of increased confidence gained through AI projects. These projects utilize AI technologies to create interactive and personalized learning experiences for black children, fostering a sense of belonging and empowerment.

Research has shown that when black children engage with AI-powered educational tools, they experience improved academic performance and enhanced self-esteem.

AI projects designed specifically for black children address their unique needs and challenges, providing culturally relevant content that reflects their identities and experiences. By incorporating diverse voices, perspectives, and narratives into the AI algorithms, these projects ensure representation and create an inclusive learning environment where black children can see themselves reflected positively.

Furthermore, AI-powered platforms offer personalized feedback and adaptive learning pathways tailored to each child's individual strengths and weaknesses. This individualized approach not only helps to bridge educational gaps but also boosts confidence as children witness their own progress.

In addition to academic benefits, AI projects empower black children by promoting critical thinking skills and encouraging them to explore new ideas independently. Through engaging with AI technologies, they develop problem-solving abilities while gaining a deeper understanding of complex concepts.

Overall, the power of AI in empowering black children lies in its ability to provide personalized learning experiences that cater to their specific needs while fostering a sense of belonging within the educational landscape.

Inspiring Black Children to Explore AI and Boost Confidence

Inspiring young individuals from the black community to engage with artificial intelligence can have a significant impact on their confidence levels. By introducing them to AI projects and encouraging their active participation, these children gain a sense of belonging and empowerment within the field. The potential for personal growth and achievement that accompanies such engagement fosters an environment where they feel valued and capable.

Artificial intelligence enables these young individuals to challenge themselves intellectually, allowing them to develop critical thinking skills while exploring innovative ideas. Through AI projects, they are exposed to various aspects of problem-solving, data analysis, and programming, which not only enhances their technical abilities but also builds their self-assurance in tackling complex challenges.

Furthermore, engaging with AI exposes these children to diverse perspectives and experiences within the field. This exposure helps foster a sense of belonging by providing opportunities for collaboration with like-minded individuals who share similar interests. By being part of a supportive community that encourages exploration and innovation in AI, these young individuals feel empowered and validated in pursuing their passions.

Building Self-Esteem through AI Projects for Black Children

Engagement in artificial intelligence initiatives offers black youth the opportunity to cultivate self-esteem and personal growth. Through participation in AI projects, black children can not only develop their technical skills but also gain confidence in their abilities. This can have a transformative impact on their sense of self and their aspirations for the future.

- **Exposure to cutting-edge technology**: Engaging with AI allows black children to familiarize themselves with advanced technologies that are shaping the world around them. By working on AI projects, they can learn about machine learning algorithms, data analysis techniques, and programming languages, which can boost their confidence in navigating the digital landscape.
- **Problem-solving and critical thinking**: AI projects often require participants to think critically and creatively to solve complex problems. Black children who engage in these initiatives learn valuable problem-solving skills that not only enhance their academic performance but also build their self-esteem as they see themselves successfully overcoming challenges.
- **Collaboration and community**: Participating in AI projects provides black children with opportunities to collaborate with peers who share similar interests. This sense of belonging within a community of like-minded individuals fosters positive relationships and creates a supportive environment where participants can feel valued and accepted.

Overcoming Challenges and Fostering Confidence with AI for Black Children

Overcoming challenges and fostering confidence can be facilitated through the participation of black youth in artificial intelligence initiatives. These initiatives provide a platform for black children to engage with cutting-edge technology, develop valuable skills, and gain recognition for their abilities. By actively involving themselves in AI projects, black children have the opportunity to confront obstacles and build resilience, which can contribute to their overall self-esteem.

Participation in AI initiatives allows black youth to overcome challenges by providing them with a supportive environment that encourages collaboration and problem-solving. Through these projects, they learn how to navigate complex tasks, analyze data, and develop innovative solutions. This hands-on experience enhances their technical skills while also instilling a sense of accomplishment and confidence in their abilities.

Furthermore, the recognition received from participating in AI projects can significantly impact the self-esteem of black children. When their talents are acknowledged and appreciated within these communities, it fosters a sense of belonging and validation. This recognition not only boosts their confidence but also empowers them to pursue further opportunities in the field.

Overall, engaging in artificial intelligence initiatives offers black youth an avenue for personal growth as they tackle challenges head-on and gain confidence through their achievements. By actively participating in these endeavors, they cultivate valuable skills while also developing a strong sense of belonging within the AI community.

Black Excellence in AI: Stories of Confidence and Success

An examination of the achievements and successes of individuals from underrepresented backgrounds in the field of artificial intelligence highlights their remarkable contributions to the advancement of AI technology. These individuals have not only overcome significant challenges but have also excelled in their respective fields, showcasing their exceptional talent and dedication. Their stories serve as an inspiration for others who may feel marginalized or underrepresented in the industry.

- **Breakthrough Innovations**: Individuals from underrepresented backgrounds have made groundbreaking innovations in AI, introducing novel algorithms and techniques that have revolutionized the field. Their contributions have expanded the boundaries of what is possible with AI technology.
- **Leadership Roles**: Many individuals from underrepresented backgrounds have assumed leadership positions within organizations working on AI projects. By taking on these roles, they bring diverse perspectives and experiences to decision-making processes, fostering inclusivity and equity within the industry.
- **Mentorship and Advocacy**: Recognizing the importance of representation, many successful individuals from underrepresented backgrounds actively mentor aspiring AI professionals and advocate for diversity in tech. By sharing their knowledge and experiences, they empower others to pursue careers in AI, creating a more inclusive environment.

These achievements demonstrate that despite facing systemic barriers, individuals from underrepresented backgrounds can excel in the field of artificial intelligence and make significant contributions to its advancement.

Frequently Asked Questions

How Does AI Technology Specifically Empower Black Children?

AI technology empowers black children by providing them with opportunities to develop skills in problem-solving, critical thinking, and creativity. It enhances their self-confidence through the ability to create and contribute to projects that harness the power of AI.

What Are Some Examples of AI Projects That Have Inspired Black Children to Explore the Field?

Examples of AI projects inspiring black children to explore the field include initiatives that provide access to resources, mentorship programs, and educational workshops focused on AI. These opportunities can foster confidence and encourage exploration in the field among black children.

How Do AI Projects Help in Building Self-Esteem and Confidence for Black Children?

AI projects contribute to the development of self-esteem and confidence in black children by providing opportunities for learning, problem-solving, and creativity. Through engagement with these projects, children gain a sense of accomplishment and empowerment, fostering their personal growth and overall well-being.

What Are Some Common Challenges That Black Children Face When Engaging with AI Projects, and How Can They Be Overcome?

Common challenges faced by black children in engaging with AI projects include limited access to resources, underrepresentation in the field, and bias in algorithms. Overcoming these challenges requires equitable access to education, diverse representation, and inclusive design practices.

Can You Share Some Success Stories of Black Children Who Have Excelled in AI Projects and Gained Confidence Through Their Achievements?

The successes of black children in AI projects have resulted in increased confidence. These achievements showcase their ability to overcome challenges and excel in this field, fostering a sense of belonging and empowerment.

Conclusion

In the realm of empowering black children, AI has emerged as a formidable ally. Through inspiring projects and exploration of AI, these young minds are discovering newfound confidence and self-esteem.

By overcoming challenges and embracing the potential of AI, black children are paving their own path towards success. Their stories exemplify the essence of black excellence in AI, where confidence is nurtured, and dreams become tangible realities.

Like a beacon in the night, AI illuminates their journey, guiding them towards a future filled with limitless possibilities.

CHAPTER 5: NAVIGATING ETHICAL AND SOCIAL IMPLICATIONS

Ethical Considerations Related to AI, Such as Bias, Privacy, and Algorithmic Accountability

In the realm of artificial intelligence (AI), ethical considerations play a crucial role in ensuring fair and responsible use of this technology. As AI systems become increasingly integrated into various aspects of our lives, it is imperative to address issues such as bias, privacy, and algorithmic accountability.

This section aims to introduce these ethical concerns, shedding light on their potential impact and exploring strategies for promoting fairness and transparency in AI systems. By examining the complexities surrounding AI development, we can strive towards a more inclusive and ethically sound future.

Key Takeaways

- Bias in AI systems can lead to discriminatory outcomes, and it can arise from biased training data, biased algorithms, or biased human input during system development.
- Privacy concerns in AI arise due to the vast amount of data collected and processed, and organizations must adopt transparent practices and obtain clear consent from individuals before collecting personal information.
- Algorithmic accountability is crucial for addressing bias, privacy, and transparency in AI systems, and it requires clear guidelines and regulations, independent audits, explainability techniques, and mechanisms for challenging and appealing AI decisions.
- Ethical challenges in AI development include perpetuating societal biases, protecting individuals' privacy rights, and ensuring fairness and transparency in AI applications such as hiring processes, criminal justice systems, and loan approvals. Strict regulations regarding data privacy can help mitigate these challenges.

The Impact of Bias in AI

The impact of bias in AI is a significant concern that raises ethical considerations related to fairness and equity. Bias refers to the systematic errors or prejudices that emerge in AI systems, influencing the outcomes and decisions they make. These biases can arise from various sources, such as biased training data, biased algorithms, or biased human input during system development. The consequences of bias in AI can be far-reaching and may perpetuate societal inequalities.

One area where bias in AI has been observed is with facial recognition systems. Studies have shown that these systems tend to exhibit higher error rates when identifying individuals from certain racial or ethnic backgrounds compared to others. This raises concerns about discrimination and unequal treatment based on race or ethnicity.

Another domain where bias has been evident is in hiring practices facilitated by AI algorithms. These algorithms can inadvertently learn biases present in historical hiring data, leading to discriminatory outcomes when selecting candidates for job interviews or making employment decisions. This not only perpetuates existing social biases but also hampers opportunities for underrepresented groups.

Addressing the impact of bias in AI requires a comprehensive approach involving diverse teams during system development, rigorous testing procedures, and ongoing monitoring for potential biases post-deployment. Additionally, transparency and accountability are essential for ensuring fairness and equity within AI systems. By recognizing the significance of bias in AI and actively working towards its mitigation, we can strive towards more inclusive technological advancements that foster belongingness for all individuals regardless of their background.

Safeguarding Privacy in an AI-driven World

Safeguarding privacy in a world driven by artificial intelligence necessitates comprehensive measures to protect individuals' personal information from unauthorized access and misuse. As AI technology continues to advance, it poses various challenges to maintaining privacy. The vast amount of data collected and processed by AI systems increases the risk of unauthorized access and potential misuse. To address these concerns, robust privacy protection mechanisms need to be implemented.

One approach is the use of encryption techniques to secure sensitive data during transmission and storage. This ensures that even if unauthorized entities gain access, they would not be able to decipher the information. Additionally, strict access controls should be employed to limit who can view or manipulate personal data within an AI system.

Furthermore, organizations must adopt transparent practices regarding their data collection and usage policies. Clear consent should be obtained from individuals before collecting their personal information, ensuring they are aware of how their data will be used.

Understanding Algorithmic Accountability

Understanding algorithmic accountability necessitates a comprehensive examination of the mechanisms and processes through which algorithms make decisions, in order to ensure transparency and fairness in their outcomes. As artificial intelligence (AI) systems become increasingly prevalent in various aspects of our lives, it is crucial to address ethical considerations such as bias, privacy, and accountability.

- **Bias**: Algorithms can perpetuate societal biases if not properly designed and monitored. This can result in unfair treatment or discrimination based on factors such as race, gender, or socioeconomic status.
- **Privacy**: AI systems often rely on vast amounts of personal data for training and decision-making. Protecting individuals' privacy rights becomes paramount to prevent unauthorized access or misuse of sensitive information.
- **Accountability**: Holding algorithms accountable for their actions raises questions

about legal responsibility and the ability to challenge automated decisions that may have significant consequences for individuals.

- **Transparency**: Ensuring transparency in algorithmic decision-making processes allows users to understand how decisions are made and identify potential biases or errors.

Ethical Challenges in AI Development

Ethical challenges arise in the development of artificial intelligence (AI) due to the potential perpetuation of societal biases and the need to protect individuals' privacy rights.

As AI systems become increasingly integrated into various aspects of society, concerns about the ethical implications they pose have gained prominence. One significant challenge is the potential for AI algorithms to perpetuate existing societal biases. Since these algorithms are trained on historical data that may contain biased information, they can inadvertently reinforce discriminatory practices or decisions. This raises questions about fairness and equity in AI applications, particularly in areas such as hiring processes, criminal justice systems, and loan approvals.

Another important ethical consideration is the protection of individuals' privacy rights. With AI's capacity to gather vast amounts of personal data from various sources, there is a growing concern about how this information is collected, stored, and used. Protecting individuals' privacy becomes crucial as AI technologies advance and become more pervasive in our daily lives.

In order to address these ethical challenges, it is imperative to develop robust mechanisms for algorithmic accountability in AI systems. This involves ensuring transparency and explainability in how decisions are made by AI algorithms so that biases can be identified and corrected when necessary. Additionally, implementing strict regulations regarding data privacy can help safeguard individuals' rights while allowing for responsible development and deployment of AI technologies.

Overall, addressing ethical challenges in the development of AI requires a comprehensive approach that considers both societal biases perpetuated by AI systems and the protection of individuals' privacy rights. By promoting fairness, equity, transparency, and accountability within AI frameworks, we can strive towards inclusive technological advancements that benefit all members of society while minimizing harm.

Promoting Fairness and Transparency in AI Systems

Promoting fairness and transparency in AI systems necessitates the implementation of measures that ensure equal treatment and provide clear explanations for decision-making processes. To achieve these goals, several key steps can be taken:

- **Developing unbiased algorithms**: Bias in AI systems can lead to unfair outcomes, disproportionately impacting certain groups or individuals. By designing algorithms that are free from bias and discrimination, fairness can be ensured.
- **Enhancing data diversity**: Diverse datasets are essential for creating inclusive AI systems. Collecting data from a wide range of sources and perspectives helps to reduce biases and improve accuracy.
- **Implementing explainability methods**: Transparency is crucial for establishing trust in AI systems. Techniques such as algorithmic explainability and interpretability enable users to understand how decisions are made, promoting

accountability.

- **Engaging diverse stakeholders**: Inclusion of diverse perspectives is essential for building fair AI systems. Engaging various stakeholders, including researchers, policymakers, industry experts, and affected communities fosters collaboration and ensures a more comprehensive approach.

Frequently Asked Questions

How Can AI Systems Be Biased, and What Are the Potential Consequences of Bias in AI?

AI systems can be biased due to the data they are trained on, the algorithms used, or the design choices made. The potential consequences of bias in AI include perpetuating social inequalities and discrimination, undermining trust in AI systems, and reinforcing harmful stereotypes.

What Measures Can Be Taken to Ensure Privacy Is Protected in an AI-Driven World?

To ensure privacy in an AI-driven world, measures such as data anonymization, encryption, and user consent should be implemented. Additionally, transparent policies on data collection and storage, as well as independent audits of AI systems, can enhance accountability and protect individuals' privacy.

Who Should Be Held Accountable for the Decisions Made by AI Algorithms, and What Steps Can Be Taken to Ensure Algorithmic Accountability?

Accountability for AI algorithms and steps towards algorithmic accountability are crucial. Identifying responsible parties, implementing transparency and auditability measures, and establishing regulatory frameworks can help ensure that decisions made by AI algorithms are fair, unbiased, and ethically accountable.

What Ethical Challenges Arise During the Development of AI Systems, and How Can These Challenges Be Addressed?

Ethical challenges in AI development include bias, privacy concerns, and algorithmic accountability. Addressing these challenges requires unbiased data collection, robust privacy protection measures, and transparent decision-making processes to ensure fairness and accountability.

How Can Fairness and Transparency Be Promoted in AI Systems, and What Are the Benefits of Doing So?

Fairness and transparency can be promoted in AI systems through the implementation of unbiased algorithms, robust privacy measures, and increased algorithmic accountability. The benefits include reducing discrimination, improving trustworthiness, and enhancing societal well-being.

Conclusion

In conclusion, ethical considerations related to AI, such as bias, privacy, and algorithmic accountability, are crucial for ensuring fairness and transparency in AI systems.

The impact of bias in AI can lead to discriminatory outcomes, highlighting the need for unbiased algorithms.

Safeguarding privacy is essential in an AI-driven world where personal data is collected and analyzed extensively.

Understanding algorithmic accountability promotes responsible use of AI technology.

With ethical challenges in AI development addressed, a statistic that highlights the significance of these considerations is that 81% of people believe that companies should be legally required to explain how they use personal data (Edelman Trust Barometer).

This statistic emphasizes the importance of transparency and accountability in ensuring public trust in AI systems.

Age-Appropriate Ways to Teach Children about the Complex Topics of Bias, Privacy, and Algorithmic Accountability

In today's technologically advanced society, it is crucial to equip children with the necessary knowledge and skills to navigate complex topics such as bias, privacy, and algorithmic accountability.

By understanding the underlying mechanisms behind these issues, children can develop critical thinking abilities and become active participants in shaping a fair and inclusive digital landscape.

This section explores age-appropriate ways to teach children about these topics, aiming to foster their understanding of biases, empower them to safeguard personal information, demystify algorithms' decision-making processes, promote fairness through algorithmic accountability awareness, and nurture ethical digital citizenship.

Key Takeaways
- Create a safe and inclusive environment for children to express their thoughts and opinions.
- Utilize diverse learning materials that represent a wide range of voices and experiences.
- Teach practical skills like setting strong passwords and adjusting privacy settings on social media platforms.
- Empower children to question and evaluate algorithmic outcomes.

Understanding Bias: Teaching Children to Recognize and Challenge Prejudices

Recognizing and challenging prejudices is an essential skill that can be taught to children as a means of understanding bias. By introducing children to the concept of bias, educators can help them develop critical thinking skills and cultivate empathy towards others. Teaching children about biases from an early age allows them to understand that biases are not inherent, or natural but rather learned behaviors influenced by societal norms and stereotypes.

To teach children about bias, it is important to use language appropriate for an audience that desires belonging. Educators should create a safe and inclusive environment where children feel comfortable expressing their thoughts and opinions without fear of judgment or ridicule. This fosters open dialogue and encourages children to question their own beliefs and assumptions.

Engaging children in interactive activities such as role-playing scenarios or storytelling can also be effective in helping them recognize biases. By presenting different perspectives and challenging stereotypes, these activities encourage critical thinking skills while promoting empathy and understanding.

Furthermore, educators should utilize diverse learning materials that represent a wide range of voices, cultures, and experiences. This helps expose children to different perspectives and reduces the reinforcement of biased attitudes.

Safeguarding Privacy: Empowering Children to Protect Their Personal Information

To ensure the safeguarding of privacy, it is imperative to equip individuals with the necessary knowledge and skills to effectively protect their personal information. In today's digital age, where personal data can be easily accessed and exploited, it is crucial for children to understand the importance of privacy and how to maintain it.

Educating children about the potential risks associated with sharing personal information online can help empower them to make informed decisions about what they share and with whom.

One age-appropriate way to teach children about safeguarding privacy is through interactive activities that encourage critical thinking and decision-making. For example, educators can engage students in discussions and role-playing scenarios that explore different online situations where personal information may be at risk. This approach allows children to actively participate in examining potential consequences and developing strategies for protecting their privacy.

Additionally, providing children with practical skills such as setting strong passwords, recognizing phishing attempts, and adjusting privacy settings on social media platforms can further enhance their ability to protect their personal information. By equipping children with these skills from a young age, they are better prepared to navigate an increasingly interconnected world while maintaining control over their own digital footprint.

Demystifying Algorithms: Explaining How Technology Makes Decisions

Algorithms, as computational processes that utilize data to make decisions, play a significant role in shaping various aspects of modern technology. Understanding how algorithms work is crucial in today's digital age. Here are three key points to consider:

1. Algorithmic decision-making: Algorithms are sets of instructions that follow predefined rules to process input and generate output. They can be found in search engines, social media platforms, recommendation systems, and more. Explaining how these algorithms function helps individuals comprehend the basis for the decisions made by technology.
2. Bias and fairness: Algorithms can perpetuate bias if they are not designed with fairness in mind or if they use biased data during their training phase. By explaining this concept to children, we can help them understand the importance of designing algorithms that treat everyone fairly and equitably.
3. Transparency and accountability: It is essential to discuss algorithmic accountability with children so that they understand the potential consequences of relying on automated decision-making systems blindly. Teaching them about transparency measures such as explainability and auditability will empower them to question and evaluate algorithmic outcomes.

Promoting Fairness: Teaching Children About Algorithmic Accountability

Promoting fairness in the digital age involves educating young individuals about the ethical implications and potential consequences of automated decision-making systems. It is crucial to teach children about algorithmic accountability in a way that is age-appropriate and fosters a sense of belonging within their communities. By doing so, we can empower them to critically analyze and navigate the complexities of biased algorithms, privacy concerns, and the need for transparency.

To effectively teach children about algorithmic accountability, educators should employ pedagogical strategies that promote engagement and understanding. This may include interactive activities that allow students to explore how algorithms work and make decisions. Additionally, discussions centered on real-life examples can help children understand the potential biases embedded within these systems.

Furthermore, it is important to emphasize the social impact of algorithmic decision-making.

Children should be encouraged to consider how these technologies can perpetuate existing inequalities or discriminate against certain groups. By highlighting these issues, educators can instill a sense of responsibility in young individuals to advocate for fairer algorithms and demand greater transparency from technology companies.

Teaching algorithmic accountability also requires creating an inclusive learning environment where all students feel valued and understood. Educators should acknowledge diverse perspectives and experiences when discussing bias, privacy, and fairness in algorithmic systems. This approach creates an atmosphere of belonging where students are more likely to actively participate in discussions and feel empowered to challenge discriminatory practices.

Nurturing Digital Citizenship: Guiding Children to Be Ethical and Responsible Online

Nurturing digital citizenship involves guiding young individuals to develop ethical and responsible behavior when engaging online. This is crucial in a world where technology plays an increasingly significant role in our daily lives. To promote digital citizenship, educators can employ age-appropriate strategies that foster a sense of belonging while teaching children about complex topics such as bias, privacy, and algorithmic accountability.

1. Cultivating empathy: Encouraging children to consider the perspectives and experiences of others helps them understand the impact of their online actions. By fostering empathy, educators can help students navigate online spaces with sensitivity towards diverse voices and backgrounds.
2. Building critical thinking skills: Teaching children to question the information they encounter online enables them to distinguish between reliable sources and misinformation. Educators can engage students in discussions where they critically analyze content for biases or inaccuracies, empowering them to make informed decisions.
3. Promoting responsible digital footprints: Children need guidance in understanding the implications of their online presence. Educators can teach them about privacy settings, appropriate sharing practices, and the potential consequences of their actions online. By emphasizing responsible digital footprints, young individuals are more likely to engage responsibly with technology while protecting their personal information.

Frequently Asked Questions

How Can Children Be Taught About the Impact of Bias on Decision-Making Processes?

The impact of bias on decision-making processes can be taught to children by introducing the concept of bias, explaining its potential consequences, and providing examples that illustrate how bias can influence decisions.

What Are Some Practical Strategies for Children to Protect Their Personal Information Online?

Practical strategies for children to protect their personal information online include teaching them about the importance of strong passwords, avoiding sharing sensitive data, being cautious with social media, and using privacy settings effectively.

How Can Parents and Educators Explain Complex Algorithms in a Way That Children Can Understand?

Explaining complex algorithms to children requires age-appropriate strategies that foster understanding. This can involve using relatable examples, visual aids, and simplified language to break down the concepts in a manner suitable for their cognitive abilities.

What Are Some Examples of Algorithmic Accountability in Everyday Life That Children Can Relate To?

Examples of algorithmic accountability in everyday life that children can relate to include personalized recommendations on streaming platforms, targeted advertisements on social media, and content filtering on search engines. These experiences can serve as starting points for discussing the concept with children.

How Can Children Be Encouraged to Practice Ethical Behavior and Responsible Online Citizenship?

Encouraging children to practice ethical behavior and responsible online citizenship can be achieved through age-appropriate education that emphasizes the importance of privacy, teaches about bias, and fosters awareness of algorithmic accountability in a manner suitable for their cognitive development.

Conclusion

In conclusion, it is crucial to teach children about the complex topics of bias, privacy, and algorithmic accountability in age-appropriate ways.

By recognizing and challenging prejudices, children can develop a sense of empathy and understanding towards others.

Empowering children to protect their personal information fosters a sense of responsibility and awareness in the digital world.

Explaining how technology makes decisions helps demystify algorithms and promotes critical thinking skills.

Teaching children about algorithmic accountability ensures fairness in decision-making processes.

One hypothetical example could be discussing with children how social media algorithms may prioritize certain posts over others based on user preferences, leading to potential echo chambers and limited exposure to diverse perspectives.

The Role of AI Education in Creating Responsible and Informed AI Users

With the rapid advancement of artificial intelligence (AI) technology, it has become crucial to emphasize the role of AI education in creating responsible and informed AI users.

As AI systems increasingly shape various aspects of our lives, it is essential for individuals to possess the necessary knowledge and skills to make ethical decisions regarding their use.

This section highlights the importance of AI education in developing critical thinking abilities, promoting transparency and accountability in AI systems, and fostering a culture of lifelong learning to ensure responsible and informed engagement with this transformative technology.

Key Takeaways

- AI education develops ethical decision-making abilities.
- AI education helps recognize biases and discriminatory practices in AI algorithms.
- AI education promotes a critical mindset in questioning underlying assumptions and values in AI systems.
- AI education enables responsible choices regarding personal data and advocates for transparency.

The Importance of AI Education in Ethical Decision-Making

The significance of AI education lies in its contribution to the development of ethical decision-making abilities among individuals using artificial intelligence. As AI technology becomes more prevalent in various aspects of our lives, it is crucial for individuals to understand the ethical implications and make informed decisions when interacting with AI systems. AI education provides individuals with the knowledge and skills necessary to navigate complex ethical dilemmas that arise in the context of artificial intelligence.

One key reason why AI education is important for ethical decision-making is that it helps individuals recognize potential biases and discriminatory practices embedded within AI algorithms. By understanding how these biases can impact decision-making processes, individuals can actively work towards mitigating them and ensuring fairness and equity in AI applications. Moreover, AI education equips individuals with a critical mindset, enabling them to question the underlying assumptions and values that shape AI systems.

Furthermore, AI education fosters an understanding of privacy concerns and data protection issues related to artificial intelligence. Individuals who are educated about these matters are more likely to make responsible choices regarding their personal data while engaging with AI technologies. They can also advocate for transparent data practices and policies that prioritize user privacy.

Understanding the Potential Risks and Benefits of AI

Understanding the potential risks and benefits of artificial intelligence requires a comprehensive assessment of its ethical implications and societal impact.

Artificial Intelligence (AI) has the capacity to revolutionize various sectors, such as healthcare, transportation, and finance. However, it also presents significant challenges that need to be addressed.

One potential risk associated with AI is job displacement, as automation could lead to unemployment for certain industries. Additionally, there are concerns about privacy and data security, as AI systems require vast amounts of personal information to function effectively. Moreover, biases embedded in AI algorithms can perpetuate existing societal inequalities if not properly addressed.

On the other hand, AI also offers numerous benefits. It can enhance efficiency and productivity by automating repetitive tasks and improving decision-making processes through advanced analytics. In healthcare, for instance, AI-powered diagnostic systems can aid in early detection of diseases and assist doctors in providing accurate treatment plans.

To fully understand these risks and benefits, it is crucial to consider the ethical implications surrounding AI development and deployment. Transparency in algorithmic decision-making processes should be promoted to ensure accountability while safeguarding individual rights and societal values.

Developing Critical Thinking Skills for Responsible AI Use

Developing critical thinking skills is essential for effectively evaluating the ethical implications and potential consequences of using artificial intelligence (AI). AI technologies are increasingly being integrated into various aspects of our lives, from healthcare to transportation. Therefore, it is crucial that individuals possess the ability to critically analyze and assess the impact of AI on society.

To foster responsible AI use, individuals should develop the following critical thinking skills:

- **Analytical Thinking**: This skill involves examining information objectively and identifying patterns or connections. By applying analytical thinking, one can better understand how AI systems work and anticipate their potential effects.
- **Ethical Reasoning**: Ethical reasoning allows individuals to consider the moral implications of using AI. It involves evaluating whether an action or decision involving AI aligns with ethical principles such as fairness, transparency, and privacy.
- **Problem Solving**: Problem-solving skills enable individuals to identify potential issues or risks associated with AI applications. By analyzing complex situations and employing creative problem-solving techniques, one can navigate ethical dilemmas that may arise in relation to AI use.

Promoting Transparency and Accountability in AI Systems

Promoting transparency and accountability in AI systems requires the establishment of clear standards and guidelines for data collection, algorithmic decision-making, and model evaluation. Transparency is essential to build trust among users and stakeholders, as it allows for a better understanding of how AI systems operate. This can be achieved through providing detailed documentation on data sources, preprocessing methods, and feature selection processes. Additionally, comprehensive explanations of algorithms used for decision-making should be made available to ensure that the outcomes are fair and unbiased.

Accountability is equally important in ensuring responsible use of AI systems. Guidelines must be established to enable the identification of responsibility when errors or biases occur. This includes defining who is accountable for system failures, addressing issues regarding liability, privacy concerns, and potential harm caused by AI decisions.

To foster transparency and accountability, collaboration between industry professionals, policymakers, researchers, and users is necessary. Public input should be sought during the development process to ensure diverse perspectives are considered. Furthermore, an open dialogue between developers and users can help address concerns about privacy breaches or biased outcomes.

Overall, promoting transparency and accountability in AI systems necessitates clear standards that encompass data collection practices as well as algorithmic decision-making processes. By adhering to these guidelines collaboratively developed by various stakeholders involved in the field of AI research and development ensures a sense of belonging amongst those interested in responsible AI use.

Fostering a Culture of Lifelong Learning in AI Education

To foster a culture of lifelong learning in the field of AI education, it is important to establish mechanisms for continuous professional development and knowledge sharing among practitioners and researchers. This will enable individuals to stay updated with the latest advancements in AI technology and techniques, ensuring that they are equipped with the necessary skills to navigate this rapidly evolving field.

- Encourage participation in conferences, workshops, and seminars: These events provide opportunities for professionals to exchange ideas, share their research findings, and learn from experts in the field. By attending such gatherings, practitioners and researchers can expand their knowledge base and gain insights into emerging trends and best practices.
- Facilitate online communities and forums: Creating online platforms where professionals can engage in discussions, ask questions, seek advice, and share resources fosters a sense of community within the AI education sector. This enables individuals to connect with like-minded peers from around the world, building networks that support ongoing learning.
- Promote collaboration between academia and industry: Establishing partnerships between educational institutions and industry organizations encourages the transfer of knowledge from research settings to real-world applications. This collaboration facilitates the integration of practical experiences into academic curricula while also providing researchers with access to valuable insights from industry professionals.

Frequently Asked Questions

How Can AI Education Help Individuals Make Ethical Decisions in Real-World Scenarios?

AI education plays a crucial role in enabling individuals to make ethical decisions in real-world scenarios. By providing knowledge and understanding of AI principles, algorithms, and their potential impacts, it empowers users to critically analyze and navigate ethical challenges posed by AI technologies.

What Are Some Potential Risks and Benefits of AI That Individuals Should Be Aware Of?

Some potential risks of AI that individuals should be aware of include job displacement, privacy concerns, and biases in decision-making. On the other hand, benefits of AI include improved efficiency, medical advancements, and enhanced personalized experiences.

What Specific Critical Thinking Skills Should Individuals Develop in Order to Use AI Responsibly?

Individuals must develop critical thinking skills to use AI responsibly. These skills include evaluating information sources, assessing potential biases in algorithms, understanding the limitations of AI systems, and recognizing ethical implications of AI applications.

How Can Transparency and Accountability Be Promoted in AI Systems to Ensure Ethical Use?

Transparency and accountability in AI systems can be promoted through measures such as clear documentation of algorithms, external audits, and public accessibility to information. These actions ensure ethical use and enhance trust among users.

What Strategies Can Be Employed to Foster a Culture of Lifelong Learning in AI Education?

Strategies for fostering a culture of lifelong learning in AI education include promoting continuous professional development, providing accessible and diverse learning resources, encouraging collaboration and knowledge-sharing among learners, and integrating real-world applications into the curriculum.

Conclusion

In conclusion, AI education plays a crucial role in shaping responsible and informed AI users.

By equipping individuals with the knowledge to understand the potential risks and benefits of AI, fostering critical thinking skills, promoting transparency and accountability in AI systems, and instilling a culture of lifelong learning, we can ensure that AI is used ethically and responsibly.

Just like a skilled navigator who charts their course through stormy seas using accurate maps and reliable instruments, educated AI users navigate the complexities of AI technology with confidence and foresight.

How Black Children, equipped with AI Knowledge, Can Contribute to More Ethical AI Systems

One potential objection to the idea of exploring how black children, equipped with AI knowledge, can contribute to more ethical AI systems may be the assumption that their involvement is unnecessary or insignificant.

However, this section aims to highlight the importance of AI education for black children and demonstrate how their diverse perspectives can address bias in AI systems.

By empowering black children to become AI creators and innovators, we can build a more inclusive AI ecosystem that considers ethical considerations in their education.

This section seeks to engage an audience interested in fostering belonging and inclusivity within the realm of AI development.

Key Takeaways

- AI education for black children fosters understanding and proficiency in AI, promoting inclusivity, diversity, and innovation in the field.
- Diverse perspectives in AI systems help identify and mitigate biases, challenge dominant narratives, and enhance accuracy and fairness.
- Empowering black children to become AI creators and innovators requires equal access to resources, quality STEM education, mentorship, and financial support.
- Involving black youth in the development of AI technologies ensures diverse perspectives are represented, provides accessible education, and creates platforms for showcasing talent and forming partnerships.

The Importance of AI Education for Black Children

The significance of providing AI education to black children lies in fostering their understanding and proficiency in the field, enabling them to actively engage in the development and implementation of more ethical AI systems. By equipping black children with AI knowledge, they are empowered to participate meaningfully in shaping the future of technology.

AI education for black children is important because it promotes inclusivity and diversity within the field. Historically, marginalized communities have been underrepresented in technological advancements, leading to biases and disparities in AI systems. By educating black children about AI, we can bridge this gap and ensure that their perspectives are considered when designing algorithms and creating AI applications.

Moreover, providing AI education to black children encourages innovation and creativity. It creates opportunities for them to explore their interests, develop critical thinking skills, and contribute fresh ideas to the field. This fosters a sense of belonging as they realize their potential impact on society through technological advancements.

Furthermore, by engaging black children in AI education, we are preparing them for future career opportunities. As technology continues to advance rapidly, there will be an increasing demand for professionals skilled in AI. Equipping black children with these skills not only enhances their employment prospects but also contributes towards addressing the racial inequalities present within the tech industry.

Addressing the Bias in AI Systems Through Diverse Perspectives

Addressing bias in AI systems can be achieved by incorporating diverse perspectives. The integration of diverse perspectives is essential for creating more ethical and inclusive AI systems. By drawing from a wide range of experiences, backgrounds, and viewpoints, it becomes possible to identify and mitigate biases that may exist within AI algorithms and datasets. This is particularly important as biases can arise from the data used to train AI systems, which often reflects existing societal inequalities.

Including diverse perspectives helps to challenge dominant narratives and assumptions that may perpetuate bias. By involving individuals who have been historically marginalized or underrepresented in the development process, we can gain insights into potential biases that may have been overlooked. Furthermore, this approach promotes a greater sense of belonging within the AI community by recognizing the value of different voices and contributions.

Incorporating diverse perspectives also enhances the accuracy and fairness of AI systems. It allows for a broader range of considerations when making decisions about algorithm design, dataset selection, and model evaluation. By including individuals with different cultural backgrounds or lived experiences, we can ensure that these systems are more representative of society as a whole.

Empowering Black Children to Become AI Creators and Innovators

Empowering black children to become creators and innovators in the field of artificial intelligence requires providing them with access to resources, opportunities, and education. By equipping black children with the necessary tools, they can actively participate in shaping the development of AI technologies and contribute their unique perspectives towards creating more ethical AI systems.

To enable this empowerment, it is crucial to ensure that black children have equal access to educational resources. This includes quality STEM education programs that introduce them to AI concepts from an early age. Additionally, providing mentorship and guidance from professionals in the field can help foster their interest and confidence in pursuing AI-related careers.

Furthermore, offering scholarships and financial support for black students interested in studying AI can remove barriers to entry and promote diversity within the industry. Inclusion of diverse voices is essential for developing robust AI systems that address biases and better serve all members of society.

Creating safe spaces where black children feel a sense of belonging within the AI community is also important. Establishing networks or affinity groups that provide support, encouragement, and opportunities for collaboration can foster a sense of community among aspiring young creators.

Building a More Inclusive AI Ecosystem with Black Youth

Building a more inclusive AI ecosystem with black youth requires creating opportunities for them to actively participate in the development and application of AI technologies. By involving black children in the AI field, it fosters a sense of belonging and empowers them to contribute meaningfully to the creation of more ethical AI systems. Inclusivity ensures that diverse perspectives are represented in decision-making processes, leading to fairer outcomes and reducing bias within AI algorithms.

To build an inclusive AI ecosystem, organizations can provide accessible educational programs that introduce black youth to the fundamentals of AI. These programs should focus on developing technical skills such as coding and data analysis while also emphasizing ethical considerations in designing AI systems. Additionally, mentorship initiatives can connect black youth with experienced professionals who can guide and support them throughout their journey in the field.

Creating platforms where young black individuals can showcase their talents and ideas is crucial for fostering inclusivity. Hackathons, competitions, or conferences specifically aimed at engaging black youth allow them to demonstrate their skills and innovations while networking with like-minded individuals and industry experts.

Moreover, partnerships between academic institutions, corporations, and community organizations play a significant role in creating inclusive environments for black youth interested in AI. Collaborative efforts ensure that resources are available, access barriers are minimized, and opportunities for growth are expanded beyond traditional avenues.

Ethical Considerations in AI Education for Black Children

Ethical considerations are a crucial aspect to consider when designing educational programs for underrepresented groups in the field of artificial intelligence. In order to create an inclusive AI ecosystem, it is important to address the ethical implications and challenges that arise from educating black children about AI.

When designing AI education programs for this specific group, it is essential to ensure that the content is culturally sensitive and representative of their experiences. This includes incorporating diverse perspectives and narratives into the curriculum, as well as addressing potential biases within AI systems.

Moreover, ethical considerations also involve fostering a sense of belonging and empowerment among black children in relation to AI. Providing opportunities for them to actively engage with AI technologies can help cultivate their interest and participation in shaping more ethical AI systems. By encouraging their involvement in discussions on bias, fairness, transparency, and accountability within AI algorithms, they can contribute unique insights that may otherwise be overlooked.

Additionally, educators must be cognizant of any potential risks associated with introducing advanced technology like AI to young learners. It is vital to strike a balance between promoting critical thinking skills and ensuring responsible use of these tools. Moreover, creating safe spaces where black children feel comfortable asking questions or expressing concerns about ethics-related issues is essential.

Overall, by integrating ethical considerations into the design of educational programs for black children in the field of artificial intelligence, we can foster a sense of belonging while empowering them to contribute towards more ethical and inclusive AI systems.

Frequently Asked Questions

What Are the Specific Challenges Faced by Black Children in Accessing AI Education?

The specific challenges faced by black children in accessing AI education include limited access to resources, lack of representation and diversity in the field, systemic biases, and societal barriers that hinder their ability to pursue and excel in AI-related studies.

How Can AI Education for Black Children Help in Addressing Bias in AI Systems?

AI education for black children can address bias in AI systems by equipping them with knowledge of ethical practices and empowering them to challenge and rectify biases. This can lead to more inclusive and equitable AI systems.

What Resources or Initiatives Are Available to Empower Black Children to Become AI Creators and Innovators?

Resources and initiatives exist to empower black children as AI creators and innovators. These programs aim to provide access to AI education, technology tools, mentorship, and inclusive learning environments to foster their skills and enable their contribution towards developing more ethical AI systems.

How Can the AI Ecosystem Be Made More Inclusive for Black Youth?

To foster inclusivity in the AI ecosystem for black youth, it is crucial to create accessible resources and opportunities that empower them to become AI creators. This can be achieved through initiatives that provide education, mentorship, and platforms for their voices to be heard and valued.

What Are the Potential Ethical Issues or Concerns in Providing AI Education Specifically for Black Children?

Potential ethical issues in providing AI education for black children include reinforcing existing biases, perpetuating inequities, and neglecting culturally relevant perspectives. It is crucial to ensure inclusive and diverse curricula that empower black children to contribute to more ethical AI systems.

Conclusion

In conclusion, it is crucial to provide AI education to black children in order to foster a more inclusive and ethical AI ecosystem. By equipping them with knowledge about AI, we can address the bias in AI systems through diverse perspectives and empower them to become creators and innovators in this field.

Through their contribution, we can build more equitable and fair AI systems. An interesting statistic shows that only 2% of Google's workforce is Black (Forbes). This highlights the need for increased representation and opportunities for black youth in the AI industry.

CHAPTER 6: INSPIRING FUTURE AI LEADERS

Successful Black Individuals in AI and Technology Fields

In a rapidly evolving technological landscape, the presence and contributions of black individuals in AI and technology fields have been both significant and transformative. These individuals have emerged as pioneers, trailblazers, and inspiring leaders who challenge preconceived notions and shatter stereotypes.

Through their excellence and success stories, they not only thrive within these domains but also inspire others to pursue their passions unabatedly.

This section aims to profile successful black individuals in AI and technology fields, highlighting their accomplishments while fostering a sense of belonging among its audience.

Key Takeaways

- Successful black individuals in AI and technology fields have made remarkable advancements and contributions in areas such as computer vision, deep learning, software development, data science, and engineering.
- These pioneers and trailblazers challenge stereotypes and societal norms, showcasing exceptional skills and expertise, and inspiring aspiring black individuals in the tech industry.
- Black leaders in AI and technology revolutionize the field, foster inclusivity, and inspire a sense of community and belonging within the industry.
- The success stories of black individuals thriving in AI and technology highlight exceptional skill and expertise from diverse backgrounds, shatter stereotypes, and pave the way for others to succeed.

Pioneers in AI and Technology: Breaking Barriers

This section focuses on the pioneers in AI and technology who have successfully overcome barriers to achieve significant advancements in their respective fields. These individuals have not only made remarkable contributions but have also paved the way for others to follow.

The first pioneer we will discuss is Dr. Mark Dean, an African American computer scientist who played a crucial role in the development of the personal computer (PC). In 1981, he co-invented the IBM Personal Computer (IBM PC), which revolutionized the computing industry and became widely adopted worldwide.

Another notable figure is Dr. Fei-Fei Li, a Chinese American computer scientist known for her groundbreaking research in computer vision and artificial intelligence. She has made significant contributions to image recognition systems and played a key role in advancing deep learning techniques.

These pioneers have broken through barriers by challenging societal norms and stereotypes, showcasing their exceptional skills and expertise in their respective fields. Their achievements serve as inspiration for aspiring black individuals pursuing careers in AI and technology, fostering a sense of belonging within this community.

Trailblazers in the Tech Industry: Black Innovators

Representing a significant presence in the tech industry, black innovators have emerged as trailblazers in their respective fields. Their contributions and achievements have not only broken barriers but also inspired and empowered individuals from diverse backgrounds who desire to belong in the world of technology. These trailblazers have made remarkable advancements across various domains such as artificial intelligence (AI), software development, data science, and engineering.

For instance, Dr. Fei-Fei Li is recognized for her groundbreaking work in computer vision and AI. As a co-founder of AI4ALL, she has actively worked towards increasing diversity and inclusion within the field of AI by providing educational opportunities to underrepresented groups.

Another prominent figure is Kimberly Bryant, who founded Black Girls CODE with the aim of introducing young girls of color to coding and technology through workshops and mentorship programs.

The accomplishments of these black innovators serve as beacons of inspiration for aspiring technologists worldwide. By showcasing their expertise, leadership skills, and determination to overcome obstacles, they demonstrate that anyone with passion and dedication can excel in the tech industry. Their stories resonate with individuals seeking a sense of belonging within this field by encouraging them to pursue their dreams without limitations based on race or ethnicity.

Inspiring Black Leaders in AI and Technology

Prominent figures in the tech industry, particularly within the field of artificial intelligence and technology, have emerged as inspiring leaders through their groundbreaking contributions and accomplishments. These individuals have not only revolutionized the way we perceive and interact with technology but have also paved a path for aspiring black professionals to find belonging and success in these fields.

One such leader is Timnit Gebru, a computer scientist known for her work on bias and fairness in machine learning algorithms. Her research has shed light on the potential dangers of using AI without considering ethical implications. Gebru's influential papers and advocacy efforts have propelled discussions surrounding diversity and inclusion within tech companies.

Another inspiring figure is Fei-Fei Li, who made significant strides in computer vision research. Li's work on image recognition systems has had a profound impact on various applications, from healthcare to autonomous vehicles. Through her leadership at Stanford University's AI Lab and as co-founder of AI4ALL, an organization focused on increasing diversity in AI education, Li has actively fostered an environment of inclusivity within the field.

These leaders exemplify how black individuals can excel in AI and technology fields while simultaneously fostering a sense of community among underrepresented groups. Their achievements serve as beacons of inspiration for those seeking to belong and make their own mark in these rapidly evolving industries.

Shattering Stereotypes: Black Excellence in Tech

Shattering stereotypes, black professionals in the tech industry have demonstrated exceptional skill and expertise, challenging preconceived notions and paving the way for inclusivity and diversity within these rapidly evolving fields. This representation of black excellence in technology not only breaks down barriers but also inspires future generations to pursue their passions without limitations.

Three key aspects highlight their remarkable contributions:

- **Technical Proficiency:** Black professionals in the tech industry consistently exhibit outstanding technical proficiency, showcasing their ability to excel in areas such as artificial intelligence (AI), data science, software engineering, and cybersecurity. Their knowledge and skills contribute significantly to advancements within these domains.
- **Leadership Roles:** Black professionals are increasingly taking up leadership positions within tech companies, serving as role models for aspiring individuals from diverse backgrounds. Through their exceptional leadership qualities, they bring unique perspectives to decision-making processes while fostering a more inclusive work environment.
- **Community Engagement:** Many black professionals actively engage with various communities by organizing workshops, mentorship programs, and initiatives aimed at increasing representation in the tech industry. By sharing their experiences and providing guidance, they empower others to overcome challenges and succeed in this field.

The accomplishments of black professionals in the tech industry challenge existing stereotypes while creating a sense of belonging for individuals who aspire to enter these fields. Their achievements not only inspire but also serve as a catalyst for increased diversity and inclusivity within technology sectors.

Success Stories: Black Individuals Thriving in AI and Technology

One notable aspect of the achievements in AI and technology is the consistent demonstration of exceptional skill and expertise by individuals from diverse backgrounds. In particular, there have been several success stories highlighting the accomplishments of black individuals in these fields. These individuals have not only shattered stereotypes but also paved the way for others to succeed, fostering a sense of belonging within the AI and technology communities.

One such success story is that of Dr. Fei-Fei Li, a prominent figure in AI research. As a Chinese American woman, she has made significant contributions to computer vision and natural language processing, particularly through her work on ImageNet. Her groundbreaking research has not only advanced the field but has also inspired countless aspiring researchers from underrepresented communities.

Another remarkable individual is Timnit Gebru, an Ethiopian American computer scientist known for her expertise in ethics and bias in AI systems. Through her work at Microsoft Research and later as co-founder of Black in AI—an organization dedicated to increasing black representation—Gebru has actively championed diversity and inclusion within the AI community.

These success stories demonstrate that black individuals possess immense talent and potential within the field of AI and technology. By showcasing their achievements, we can inspire others who desire to pursue careers in these fields, ultimately leading to more diverse perspectives and innovative solutions.

Frequently Asked Questions

What Are Some of the Biggest Challenges Faced by Black Individuals in the AI and Technology Fields?

Some of the biggest challenges faced by black individuals in the AI and technology fields include underrepresentation, lack of access to resources and opportunities, bias and discrimination, stereotype threat, and limited mentorship and networking opportunities.

How Have Black Innovators Contributed to the Advancement of AI and Technology?

Black innovators have significantly contributed to the advancement of AI and technology through their groundbreaking research, inventions, and influential leadership. Their contributions have fostered progress, diversity, and inclusivity within these fields.

What Are Some of the Initiatives and Programs Aimed at Promoting Diversity and Inclusion in the AI and Technology Industries?

Promoting diversity and inclusion in the AI and technology industries involves various initiatives and programs. These aim to address underrepresentation of marginalized groups, create equal opportunities, support diverse talent, and foster inclusive work environments.

Can You Provide Examples of Black Leaders Who Have Made Significant Contributions to AI and Technology?

Significant contributions to AI and technology have been made by black leaders. These individuals have played a vital role in advancing the field through their expertise, innovation, and leadership, contributing to the overall progress and success of the industry.

How Can the Broader Tech Industry Support and Uplift Black Individuals Pursuing Careers in AI and Technology?

In order to support and uplift black individuals pursuing careers in AI and technology, the broader tech industry can implement initiatives such as mentorship programs, scholarships, and diversity training to create a more inclusive and equitable environment.

Conclusion

In conclusion, the remarkable achievements of black individuals in AI and technology fields serve as a beacon of inspiration for generations to come. They have shattered barriers and defied stereotypes, paving the way for a more inclusive and diverse industry.

Like shooting stars across a night sky, these trailblazers have ignited a passion for innovation and excellence. Their success stories remind us that talent knows no boundaries, and when given equal opportunities, brilliance can flourish in all shades.

How Early Exposure to AI Can Inspire Black Children to Pursue Careers in STEM

In a world driven by technological advancements, the symbol of early exposure to AI represents an opportunity to inspire black children in their pursuit of careers in STEM fields.

This section explores the importance of introducing AI at an early age for black children, examining how it can break barriers and empower them in their STEM journeys.

Additionally, it delves into the role of AI education in nurturing curiosity, building confidence, and creating opportunities for black children within the realm of STEM.

Key Takeaways

- Early exposure to AI can inspire black children to pursue careers in STEM by introducing them to the possibilities and opportunities in AI.
- AI education provides black children with critical thinking, problem-solving, and analytical reasoning skills, which are essential for success in STEM fields.
- AI education fosters a sense of belonging and confidence among black children by showcasing representation in AI spaces and highlighting successful individuals from their own communities as role models.
- AI education breaks down barriers in the STEM field and empowers black children by providing them with early exposure to STEM fields, engaging them in hands-on learning experiences, and offering culturally relevant content that resonates with their experiences.

The Importance of Early Exposure to AI for Black Children

The significance of providing early exposure to artificial intelligence (AI) for black children lies in its potential to inspire their pursuit of careers in STEM fields. Early exposure to AI can introduce black children to the possibilities and opportunities within the field, allowing them to develop a passion and interest from a young age. By exposing them to AI technologies and concepts, they can gain valuable skills such as critical thinking, problem-solving, and analytical reasoning.

Furthermore, early exposure to AI can help black children overcome barriers that exist within the STEM field. Historically, there has been underrepresentation of black individuals in STEM professions due to various systemic factors. However, by introducing AI at an early stage, we can empower black children with knowledge and tools that will enable them to compete on an equal footing with their peers.

Providing this early exposure also fosters a sense of belonging among black children. It sends a message that they are valued members of the STEM community and have the potential to contribute significantly. This feeling of belonging is crucial for inspiring confidence and encouraging them to pursue careers in STEM fields.

Inspiring Black Children to Pursue STEM Careers through AI

Encouraging underrepresented youth to engage with emerging technologies such as artificial intelligence can help foster their interest in science, technology, engineering, and mathematics (STEM) fields. For black children, early exposure to AI presents an opportunity to inspire them towards pursuing STEM careers. The utilization of AI in various industries and its transformative potential creates a sense of belonging for these children by highlighting the relevance of their participation in shaping the future.

By introducing AI concepts and applications at an early age, black children are exposed to a range of possibilities within STEM fields. This exposure not only helps them develop technical skills but also instills confidence in their ability to contribute meaningfully to these domains. Moreover, engaging with AI allows black children to see themselves represented within these spaces, which further enhances their sense of belonging.

Incorporating culturally relevant examples and role models in AI education can also enhance the feeling of belonging for black children. By showcasing successful individuals from their own communities who have pursued STEM careers or made significant contributions through AI technology, black children are motivated and inspired by relatable figures.

How AI Can Break Barriers and Empower Black Children in STEM

By promoting access to and utilization of artificial intelligence, barriers can be broken down for underrepresented groups in the field of STEM, such as black children. Artificial intelligence (AI) has the potential to empower black children by providing them with opportunities for early exposure to STEM fields. Early exposure to AI can inspire and encourage black children to pursue careers in STEM by fostering a sense of belonging and demonstrating their potential in these fields.

AI technologies, such as educational apps and robotics kits, can engage black children in hands-on learning experiences that are both fun and educational. These tools can help them develop critical thinking skills, problem-solving abilities, and computational thinking processes from an early age.

Additionally, AI platforms can promote inclusivity by offering culturally relevant content that resonates with black children's experiences. By incorporating diverse perspectives and narratives into AI-powered educational resources, it creates an environment where black children feel represented and valued. This sense of belonging is crucial for inspiring confidence in their abilities and encouraging them to pursue STEM careers.

Furthermore, AI-driven mentorship programs can facilitate connections between black children interested in STEM and professionals working in these fields who look like them. These mentorship relationships provide guidance, support, and role models that exemplify successful individuals who have overcome similar challenges faced by underrepresented groups. Through this mentoring process facilitated by AI technology platforms or applications, black children gain access to valuable insights about career paths within STEM disciplines.

Nurturing Curiosity and Creativity in Black Children Through AI Education

Nurturing curiosity and creativity in underrepresented groups can be facilitated through the implementation of AI education. In particular, providing Black children with early exposure to AI could significantly inspire them to pursue careers in STEM fields. By introducing AI concepts and technologies at a young age, it creates an environment that fosters curiosity and encourages exploration. This exposure allows children to develop a sense of belonging within the world of technology, empowering them to engage with STEM subjects more confidently.

AI education offers various opportunities for Black children to explore their interests and passions. It provides them with hands-on experiences in problem-solving, critical thinking, and innovation. Through interactive activities such as coding or robotics, children can unleash their creativity while simultaneously learning about the principles behind artificial intelligence.

Moreover, AI education helps dismantle any misconceptions or stereotypes surrounding STEM fields that may discourage Black children from pursuing these careers. By showcasing diverse role models who have succeeded in AI-related fields, it instills a sense of belonging and shows that anyone can thrive in these disciplines regardless of their background.

Building Confidence and Skills in Black Children with AI at an Early Age

The implementation of AI education at an early age can equip underrepresented groups, such as Black children, with the necessary confidence and skills to actively engage in technological advancements. By providing opportunities for Black children to learn about AI and its applications from a young age, they are more likely to develop a sense of belonging in the field of STEM (Science, Technology, Engineering, and Mathematics). This early exposure allows them to build the foundational knowledge required for future success.

AI education offers numerous benefits for Black children. Firstly, it fosters curiosity and sparks interest in technology-related fields. As they explore AI concepts and witness its real-world applications, their motivation to pursue careers in STEM is heightened. Additionally, early exposure to AI helps cultivate critical thinking skills and problem-solving abilities. These skills are essential for success in STEM disciplines as they encourage analytical reasoning and innovation.

Moreover, by engaging with AI at an early age, Black children can develop self-confidence in their abilities. They gain hands-on experience with cutting-edge technologies that may have previously seemed inaccessible or intimidating. This increased confidence enables them to envision themselves as active contributors within the field of technology.

Creating Opportunities for Black Children in STEM through AI Education

Creating opportunities for underrepresented groups in the field of STEM can be accomplished through the implementation of AI education at an early age. In particular, providing black children with access to AI education can inspire and encourage them to pursue careers in STEM. Historically, black individuals have been underrepresented in the field of STEM due to various systemic barriers and lack of exposure. By introducing AI education at an early age, black children can develop a strong foundation in technology and computational thinking skills. This early exposure allows them to explore their interests and talents in a supportive environment, fostering a sense of belonging and empowerment.

AI education provides numerous benefits for black children interested in pursuing careers in STEM. Firstly, it exposes them to real-world applications of technology and demonstrates its potential impact on society. This exposure helps cultivate their curiosity and passion for learning about new technologies. Additionally, AI education equips black children with valuable skills such as critical thinking, problem-solving, and data analysis. These skills are crucial for success in the modern workforce.

Furthermore, AI education promotes diversity within the field by encouraging participation from different backgrounds and perspectives. By nurturing talent among underrepresented groups like black children, it creates a more inclusive STEM community that values diversity. This not only enriches the field but also ensures that innovative solutions are developed with input from diverse voices.

Frequently Asked Questions

What Are Some Specific Examples of AI Programs or Initiatives That Have Successfully Inspired Black Children to Pursue STEM Careers?

Various AI programs and initiatives have effectively inspired black children to pursue STEM careers. For example, the "AI4ALL" organization offers summer camps and educational programs that introduce AI concepts and technologies to underrepresented communities, including black children.

Are There Any Challenges or Barriers That Black Children May Face When Trying to Access AI Education and Opportunities?

Challenges or barriers that black children may face when accessing AI education and opportunities include limited access to resources and role models, systemic inequalities in the education system, and a lack of representation in STEM fields.

How Can AI Education and Exposure Help to Address the Underrepresentation of Black Individuals in STEM Fields?

Early exposure to AI education and exposure can contribute to addressing the underrepresentation of black individuals in STEM fields by providing opportunities for skill development, fostering interest and confidence, and challenging societal stereotypes and biases.

What Are Some Potential Long-Term Benefits or Outcomes of Early Exposure to AI for Black Children?

Early exposure to AI can cultivate interest in STEM among Black children, leading to increased representation in these fields. This can foster innovation, diversity, and equitable opportunities, benefiting both individuals and society as a whole.

Are There Any Specific Strategies or Approaches That Have Been Found to Be Particularly Effective in Nurturing Curiosity and Creativity in Black Children Through AI Education?

Research has shown that specific strategies and approaches can effectively nurture curiosity and creativity in black children through AI education. These include providing hands-on experiences, incorporating culturally relevant content, and promoting collaboration and problem-solving skills.

Conclusion

In conclusion, early exposure to AI has the potential to inspire black children to pursue careers in STEM. By breaking barriers and empowering them, AI education can nurture curiosity and creativity in these children. It also builds confidence and essential skills from an early age.

Through AI education, opportunities are created for black children in the field of STEM, providing them with a pathway to success. The impact of AI on inspiring and guiding young minds towards a future in STEM cannot be underestimated.

Mentorship Programs and Initiatives That Support Young Black AI Enthusiasts

The engagement and support of young black AI enthusiasts through mentorship programs and initiatives have emerged as crucial elements in fostering their professional growth.

Through effective guidance and assistance, these programs aim to provide valuable opportunities for skill development and access to networks within the AI field.

This section explores the significance of mentorship in facilitating the advancement of young black AI enthusiasts, highlights prominent mentorship programs, discusses bridging initiatives, presents strategies for effective mentorship, shares success stories, and offers insights into future prospects for advancing diversity through mentorship in AI.

Key Takeaways

- Mentorship programs provide guidance, support, and access to resources for the professional development of young black AI enthusiasts.
- These programs address underrepresentation in the AI industry by offering insights, advice, and knowledge about the field.
- Mentors act as role models, inspiring young black enthusiasts to pursue their aspirations and overcome barriers due to lack of representation.
- Prominent mentorship programs and initiatives like Black in AI Mentoring Program, AI4ALL, Data Science Africa, and Code2040 empower young black individuals interested in AI by providing guidance, expertise, and networking opportunities.

Importance of Mentorship in AI for Young Black Enthusiasts

The significance of mentorship in the field of artificial intelligence for young black enthusiasts lies in its potential to provide guidance, support, and access to resources necessary for their professional development.

Mentorship programs and initiatives play a crucial role in addressing the underrepresentation of young black individuals in the AI industry. These programs offer a platform for aspiring professionals to connect with experienced mentors who can provide valuable insights, advice, and knowledge about the field.

Mentorship provides guidance by offering a roadmap for navigating the complexities of the AI industry. The mentor's expertise and experience help mentees understand the skills required, identify potential career paths, and set achievable goals. Mentors also act as role models, demonstrating what success looks like in AI careers and inspiring young black enthusiasts to pursue their aspirations.

Additionally, mentorship offers vital support by creating a supportive network where mentees can discuss challenges they may face along their journey. This support system encourages open communication, fosters resilience, and helps individuals overcome obstacles that may deter them from pursuing a career in AI.

Furthermore, mentorship programs grant access to resources that are essential for professional development. Mentors can provide introductions to industry professionals or institutions that offer training opportunities or scholarships specifically designed for young black individuals interested in AI. By leveraging these connections and resources provided by mentors, young black enthusiasts gain access to opportunities that might otherwise be difficult to obtain.

Prominent Mentorship Programs for Young Black AI Enthusiasts

Notable resources have been developed to provide guidance and assistance to individuals from the African Diaspora with an interest in artificial intelligence. These resources aim to create a sense of belonging and support for young black AI enthusiasts, recognizing the importance of mentorship in their professional development.

Some prominent mentorship programs for young black AI enthusiasts include:

- **Black in AI Mentoring Program**: This program connects young black AI enthusiasts with experienced professionals in the field who can provide guidance, advice, and support. Mentors help mentees navigate career opportunities, build networks, and overcome challenges they may face as minority individuals in the AI industry.
- **AI4ALL**: AI4ALL is a non-profit organization that offers summer programs for high school students from underrepresented backgrounds, including those from the African diaspora. Through hands-on learning experiences, mentorship, and exposure to cutting-edge AI research, participants gain valuable skills and knowledge while building a supportive community.
- **Data Science Africa**: Data Science Africa provides mentorship opportunities for aspiring data scientists and AI researchers across the African continent. The program aims to foster collaboration among individuals interested in machine learning and data science by connecting them with experienced practitioners who can offer guidance on research projects, career paths, and skill development.

These mentorship programs play a crucial role in empowering young black individuals interested in AI by providing access to guidance, expertise, and networks within the field.

Initiatives Bridging the Gap for Young Black AI Enthusiasts

Prominent efforts have been made to bridge the gap and provide opportunities for individuals from underrepresented backgrounds in the field of artificial intelligence. Several initiatives have emerged that aim to support young black AI enthusiasts by offering mentorship programs and other resources. These initiatives recognize the importance of diversity and inclusivity in AI and seek to address the lack of representation within the field.

One such initiative is the Black in AI (BAI) community, which focuses on fostering collaboration and networking among black professionals and students in AI. BAI organizes workshops, conferences, and mentorship programs to provide guidance and support to young black AI enthusiasts. Through these activities, BAI aims to create a sense of belonging for its members while also promoting their professional development.

Another initiative is Code2040, which works towards creating pathways into tech careers for underrepresented minorities, including those interested in AI. Code2040 offers a comprehensive fellowship program that provides both technical training and professional development opportunities. By connecting fellows with industry professionals as mentors, Code2040 aims to provide them with valuable guidance as they navigate their careers in tech.

These initiatives play a crucial role in bridging the gap for young black AI enthusiasts by offering mentorship, networking opportunities, and resources necessary for their success. By addressing barriers faced by underrepresented groups, these initiatives contribute to creating a more inclusive environment within the field of artificial intelligence.

Strategies for Effective Mentorship in the AI Field

Effective mentorship in the field of artificial intelligence involves implementing strategies that facilitate knowledge sharing, skill development, and career guidance for individuals seeking to excel in this domain. To create a sense of belonging and foster growth among mentees, mentors can employ various strategies:

- Regular one-on-one meetings: These meetings provide mentees with personalized attention and guidance. Mentors can use these sessions to discuss progress, address challenges, and provide feedback on specific projects or assignments.
- Group activities and workshops: Organizing group activities allows mentees to connect with peers who share similar interests and goals. Workshops focused on technical skills development or industry trends can enhance the learning experience by providing an interactive platform for discussion and collaboration.
- Networking opportunities: Mentors can facilitate networking events where mentees can interact with professionals from the AI industry. These opportunities allow mentees to expand their professional network, gain insights into potential career paths, and seek advice from experienced individuals.

Success Stories: Young Black AI Enthusiasts and Their Mentors

A number of success stories highlight the positive impact that mentors have had on the development and achievements of young individuals interested in artificial intelligence. These success stories serve as evidence of the effectiveness and importance of mentorship programs for young black AI enthusiasts.

For example, one success story involves a young black AI enthusiast named Jamal, who was paired with a mentor through a local AI organization. With his mentor's guidance and support, Jamal was able to navigate the complex world of AI and develop his skills in programming and machine learning. His mentor provided him with valuable resources, advice, and opportunities to network with professionals in the field. As a result, Jamal gained confidence in his abilities and went on to secure an internship at a leading technology company specializing in AI.

This success story demonstrates how mentors can provide not only technical knowledge but also empower young black AI enthusiasts by helping them overcome barriers they may face due to lack of representation in the field.

Overall, these success stories emphasize the transformative power of mentorship for young black AI enthusiasts seeking belonging and growth within the field.

Future Outlook: Advancing Diversity through Mentorship in AI

Increased diversity in the field of artificial intelligence can be advanced through the implementation of mentorship strategies that foster inclusivity and equal opportunities for underrepresented groups. Mentorship programs hold great potential to address the existing disparities by providing guidance, support, and encouragement to young black AI enthusiasts. By leveraging mentorship initiatives, the AI community can create an environment where individuals from diverse backgrounds feel valued and empowered.

Collaborative Learning Spaces: Mentorship programs can establish collaborative learning spaces where young black AI enthusiasts can engage with peers who share similar experiences and aspirations. This fosters a sense of belonging and encourages knowledge sharing, collaboration, and innovation.

Expert Guidance: Matching mentees with experienced mentors who have expertise in artificial intelligence allows mentees to receive personalized guidance on their career paths. Such expert guidance helps young black AI enthusiasts navigate challenges, gain insights into industry trends, and develop relevant skills.

Building Networks: Mentorship programs facilitate networking opportunities for mentees within the AI community. These networks provide access to resources such as internships, scholarships, or job opportunities that may otherwise be difficult to obtain.

Frequently Asked Questions

How Can Mentorship Programs Specifically Benefit Young Black AI Enthusiasts?

Mentorship programs are beneficial to young black AI enthusiasts as they provide guidance, knowledge transfer, and networking opportunities. Mentors can offer insights into the industry, help navigate challenges, and serve as role models for career aspirations.

Are There Any Mentorship Programs That Focus on Providing Financial Support for Young Black AI Enthusiasts?

Mentorship programs focusing on providing financial support for young black AI enthusiasts exist. These initiatives aim to address the specific needs of underrepresented individuals in the field, fostering their development and promoting diversity in the AI community.

What Are Some Key Challenges Faced by Young Black AI Enthusiasts in Accessing Mentorship Opportunities?

Key challenges faced by young Black AI enthusiasts in accessing mentorship opportunities include limited representation and lack of access to resources, networks, and role models. These barriers contribute to disparities in skill development and hinder their participation in the field.

How Do Initiatives Bridging the Gap for Young Black AI Enthusiasts Differ from Traditional Mentorship Programs?

Initiatives bridging the gap for young Black AI enthusiasts differ from traditional mentorship programs by specifically targeting and supporting this underrepresented group. They aim to provide tailored guidance, resources, and opportunities to address unique challenges faced by these individuals in accessing mentorship.

Can You Provide Examples of Successful Mentorship Strategies Used in the AI Field for Young Black Enthusiasts?

Examples of successful mentorship strategies in the AI field for young Black enthusiasts include targeted recruitment efforts, pairing mentees with experienced professionals, providing access to resources and networks, offering ongoing support and guidance, and fostering a sense of belonging and community.

Conclusion

In conclusion, mentorship programs and initiatives play a crucial role in supporting young black

AI enthusiasts and bridging the diversity gap in the field. By providing guidance, knowledge, and opportunities, these programs empower aspiring individuals to excel in AI.

Strategies such as creating inclusive environments, fostering strong relationships, and offering ongoing support are essential for effective mentorship. Through these efforts, we can witness success stories of young black AI enthusiasts achieving their goals with the help of their mentors.

Moving forward, it is imperative to continue advancing diversity in AI through mentorship programs that nurture talent and drive innovation. As the saying goes, 'A rising tide lifts all boats,' and by investing in mentorship opportunities for young black AI enthusiasts, we can create a more inclusive and thriving future for all.

The Potential for Black Children to Become Leaders and Innovators in the AI Industry

According to recent data, black children are significantly underrepresented in the field of artificial intelligence (AI). This lack of representation not only hinders diversity within the industry but also limits opportunities for these children to contribute as leaders and innovators.

In order to address this issue, it is crucial to nurture and encourage talent among black children in AI. By breaking barriers and empowering the next generation of black innovators, we can foster a more inclusive and diverse future for the AI industry.

Key Takeaways

- Black children have significant potential to become leaders and innovators in the AI industry.
- Inclusive AI education and access to quality resources and mentorship are crucial for nurturing this potential.
- Collaboration with schools, policymakers, and companies committed to diversity can help break down barriers and provide opportunities for black children in AI.
- Empowering black children in AI not only benefits them individually but also has wider societal benefits.

The Underrepresentation of Black Children in AI

The underrepresentation of black children in the AI industry is a pressing issue that warrants attention and intervention. Despite advancements in technology and increasing demand for diversity and inclusion, black children continue to be underrepresented in this field. This lack of representation not only limits the opportunities available to black individuals but also hinders the industry's potential for innovation.

One reason for this underrepresentation is the limited access to resources and opportunities that many black children face. Socioeconomic disparities, unequal educational systems, and systemic barriers contribute to this disadvantage. Additionally, the lack of diverse role models in the AI industry further perpetuates the notion that there is no place for black children within this field.

Addressing these challenges requires a multifaceted approach. First, it is crucial to provide equal access to quality education and resources for all children, regardless of their background. This includes creating programs that focus on STEM education specifically targeting underserved communities.

Moreover, mentorship programs can play a vital role in exposing black children to successful professionals who can inspire and guide them towards pursuing careers in AI. To foster belonging within the AI industry, organizations must prioritize diversity initiatives by actively recruiting and retaining individuals from underrepresented backgrounds.

The Importance of Diversity in the AI Industry

Diversity plays a crucial role in the AI industry, fostering innovation and enhancing problem-solving capabilities. Embracing diversity within the field not only contributes to a sense of belonging but also leads to a more comprehensive understanding and approach towards addressing complex challenges.

Here are five reasons why diversity is important in the AI industry:

- Different perspectives: Diversity brings together individuals from various backgrounds, cultures, and experiences. This diverse range of perspectives allows for a broader exploration of ideas and solutions.
- Creativity and innovation: A diverse workforce encourages creativity by promoting different ways of thinking. This enables the generation of innovative solutions that may not have been considered otherwise.
- Improved decision-making: When teams comprise individuals with diverse backgrounds, they are better equipped to consider multiple viewpoints before making decisions. This can lead to more thorough analysis and ultimately better outcomes.
- Enhanced problem-solving capabilities: Cognitive diversity, derived from a mix of skills, knowledge domains, and approaches to problem-solving, strengthens teams' abilities to tackle complex issues effectively.
- Increased market reach: By embracing diversity in the AI industry, companies can better understand and cater to the needs of diverse customer bases worldwide.

Nurturing Talent: Encouraging Black Children in AI

Nurturing and promoting inclusivity in AI education can contribute to the development of a diverse talent pool capable of driving innovation in the field. Encouraging black children to participate in AI presents an opportunity for them to become leaders and innovators, fostering their sense of belonging and empowerment within this industry.

By nurturing talent among black children in AI, we can create an environment that supports their growth and development. This involves providing access to quality education, resources, and mentorship opportunities specifically tailored to their needs. In doing so, we acknowledge the unique perspectives and experiences they bring to the table.

Inclusive AI education helps break down barriers that may hinder black children from entering this field. It sends a powerful message that their voices matter and are essential for driving innovation. By actively involving them in AI education initiatives, we can foster a sense of belonging among black children who may have previously felt excluded or marginalized.

Moreover, nurturing talent among black children in AI has wider societal benefits. It promotes diversity within the industry by bringing different perspectives, ideas, and skills to the forefront. This not only enhances problem-solving capabilities but also fosters creativity and innovation.

Breaking Barriers: Black Children as AI Leaders

Breaking barriers and promoting inclusivity in the field of artificial intelligence can empower underrepresented individuals to take on leadership roles. This is particularly important for black children, as they face unique challenges and barriers in accessing opportunities in the AI industry. By creating an inclusive environment that values diversity, we can foster a sense of belonging and create pathways for black children to become leaders and innovators in this rapidly advancing field.

- Providing mentorship programs specifically tailored for black children interested in AI can help them navigate the industry and gain valuable skills.
- Offering scholarships and financial support to black students pursuing AI education can remove financial barriers that often limit access to these opportunities.

- Organizing networking events and conferences that bring together black professionals already working in AI can provide role models and inspiration for aspiring leaders.
- Collaborating with schools, community organizations, and policymakers to develop AI curriculum that is inclusive, culturally relevant, and accessible to all students.
- Creating partnerships with companies committed to diversity and inclusion can provide internships, job opportunities, and mentorship programs specifically targeting black children.

Empowering the Next Generation of Black Innovators in AI

To foster the growth of black talent in the field of artificial intelligence, it is crucial to establish equitable access to educational resources and opportunities. By providing a level playing field for black children, we can empower and inspire the next generation of black innovators in AI.

One key aspect of promoting equity is ensuring that quality education in AI is accessible to all students, regardless of their racial background. This includes creating inclusive curricula that reflect diverse perspectives and experiences, as well as offering scholarships or financial support for underrepresented students.

In addition to educational resources, it is essential to provide mentorship programs and networking opportunities for aspiring black AI professionals. These initiatives can help bridge the gap between academia and industry by connecting students with experienced professionals who can guide them on their career paths.

Moreover, fostering a sense of belonging within the AI community is vital. Creating safe spaces where black students feel valued and supported can enhance their confidence and motivation to pursue careers in AI. Encouraging diversity within research teams and organizations also contributes to a more inclusive environment where different viewpoints are respected and celebrated.

Ultimately, by prioritizing equitable access to education, mentorship programs, networking opportunities, and fostering a sense of belonging within the AI community, we can empower the next generation of black innovators in AI.

Frequently Asked Questions

How Can the Underrepresentation of Black Children in the AI Industry Be Addressed and Improved?

Addressing and improving the underrepresentation of black children in the AI industry requires implementing strategies that promote inclusivity, such as increasing access to educational opportunities, providing mentorship programs, and fostering a supportive environment that values diversity.

What Are Some of the Specific Benefits and Advantages of Diversity in the AI Industry?

Diversity in the AI industry offers numerous benefits and advantages. It fosters a variety of perspectives and experiences, resembling a vibrant tapestry that enriches problem-solving approaches, enhances creativity, and promotes innovation for the betterment of society.

What Initiatives or Programs Are Currently in Place to Encourage and Nurture the Talent of Black Children in the Field of AI?

Initiatives and programs are being implemented to encourage and nurture the talent of black children in AI. These efforts aim to provide equal opportunities, access to resources, mentorship, and educational support for their development in this industry.

What Barriers or Challenges Do Black Children Face When Pursuing Leadership Roles in the AI Industry, and How Can These Barriers Be Overcome?

Barriers and challenges faced by Black children in pursuing leadership roles in the AI industry include systemic racism, limited access to resources and opportunities, and lack of representation. Overcoming these barriers requires creating inclusive environments, increasing diversity in leadership positions, and providing equal access to educational resources.

What Steps Can Be Taken to Empower and Support the Next Generation of Black Innovators in the Field of AI?

Steps to empower and support the next generation of black innovators in AI include fostering inclusive educational environments, providing mentorship opportunities, promoting diversity in industry leadership, offering scholarships and internships, and advocating for equal access to resources and opportunities.

Conclusion

In conclusion, the underrepresentation of black children in the AI industry is a pressing issue that needs to be addressed. The lack of diversity not only hinders innovation but also perpetuates inequality.

By nurturing talent and breaking barriers, we have the potential to empower the next generation of black innovators in AI. It is ironic that a field driven by advancements fails to recognize the immense talent and potential within black children.

Let us strive for inclusivity and create a future where all voices are heard and celebrated in the AI industry.

CHAPTER 7: OVERCOMING CHALLENGES AND LOOKING AHEAD

Potential Challenges in Implementing AI Education, Including Access to Resources and Teacher Training for Black Children

The implementation of AI education for black children poses potential challenges that need to be addressed.

Access to adequate resources and teacher training are key factors in ensuring the effective delivery of AI education.

Limited access to AI resources highlights the need to address the digital divide, while emphasizing the importance of providing equitable opportunities for black students.

Moreover, adequate teacher training is crucial in enabling educators to effectively teach AI concepts and skills, mitigating bias and stereotypes that may hinder black children's participation in this field.

This section aims to explore strategies for empowering black children through inclusive and accessible AI education.

Key Takeaways

- Limited access to resources, such as computers, software, and high-speed internet, hinders black children's engagement with AI education.
- There is a shortage of qualified teachers with expertise in AI concepts, creating an additional barrier for black children to access quality AI education.
- Bridging the digital divide is crucial to ensure equal access to technology and internet connectivity for black children in AI education.
- Equipping educators with the necessary knowledge and skills through targeted professional development is essential for delivering high-quality AI education to black children.

Challenges in AI Education for Black Children

One of the challenges in implementing AI education for black children is the limited access to resources and teacher training. This issue creates a significant disparity in educational opportunities, hindering their ability to fully engage with AI technologies and gain necessary skills. Access to resources, such as computers, software, and high-speed internet, is essential for effective AI education. Unfortunately, many black communities lack the infrastructure and financial means to provide these resources adequately.

Moreover, teacher training plays a crucial role in delivering quality AI education. However, there is a shortage of qualified teachers who possess the expertise required to teach AI concepts effectively. Black children often face an additional barrier when it comes to accessing well-trained teachers due to systemic inequalities within the education system.

Addressing these challenges requires a comprehensive approach that focuses on improving resource accessibility and enhancing teacher training programs. Initiatives aimed at bridging the digital divide by providing equitable access to technology can significantly alleviate this problem. Additionally, investing in targeted professional development programs for teachers will ensure they have the necessary knowledge and skills to deliver high-quality AI education.

Limited Access to AI Resources

Limited access to resources hinders the effective implementation of AI education for black children. In order to fully engage with AI technology and develop the necessary skills, students require access to high-quality equipment, software, and internet connectivity. However, many African American communities face significant disparities in terms of resource allocation for education. This lack of access negatively impacts the ability of black children to participate in AI education programs.

One major challenge is the unequal distribution of funding for schools serving predominantly black students. These schools often have limited budgets, resulting in outdated technology and inadequate resources for teaching AI concepts. Additionally, there may be a shortage of qualified teachers who can effectively deliver AI education due to limited training opportunities.

Furthermore, socioeconomic factors play a significant role in limiting access to resources that facilitate AI education. Many African American families may not have the financial means to purchase expensive computers or pay for internet services at home. This creates a digital divide where black children are unable to explore and practice AI skills outside of school hours.

To address these challenges and ensure equitable access to AI resources, policymakers must prioritize investment in schools serving predominantly black communities. Efforts should focus on providing updated technology infrastructure and professional development opportunities for teachers. Additionally, initiatives aimed at bridging the digital divide through affordable internet options can help promote equal participation in AI education among all students.

Addressing the Digital Divide

Efforts to bridge the digital divide in AI education require a comprehensive approach that includes equitable distribution of funding, updated technology infrastructure, and affordable internet options for all students.

- **Equitable distribution of funding**: Ensuring that schools in underserved communities have access to sufficient funds is crucial in addressing the digital divide. This includes allocating resources specifically for AI education, such as providing funds for training teachers and purchasing necessary equipment.
- **Updated technology infrastructure**: Many schools in marginalized communities lack up-to-date technology infrastructure, hindering their ability to provide effective AI education. Investing in modern hardware and software solutions is essential to create an environment where students can learn and explore AI

technologies.

- **Affordable internet options:** Access to affordable and reliable internet is vital for students to engage with online AI resources and participate in remote learning opportunities. Providing subsidized or low-cost internet plans can help ensure that all students have equal access to the online tools and materials needed for AI education.

Importance of Teacher Training in AI Education

A comprehensive and effective approach to bridging the digital divide in AI education involves prioritizing teacher training to ensure educators have the necessary knowledge and skills to effectively teach AI concepts and technologies.

Teacher training plays a crucial role in equipping educators with the tools they need to navigate the complexities of AI education, particularly for black children who may face additional challenges in accessing resources. By providing teachers with targeted training programs, they can develop a deep understanding of AI concepts and gain proficiency in using relevant technologies.

Teacher training should focus on several key areas. First, teachers need a solid foundation in AI principles and applications so that they can effectively convey these concepts to their students. This includes understanding machine learning algorithms, neural networks, and data analysis techniques.

Second, teachers should be trained on how to integrate AI into their existing curriculum across various subjects such as mathematics, science, or social studies. This will enable them to create engaging and interdisciplinary learning experiences for their students.

Furthermore, teacher training should also address potential biases or ethical concerns related to AI systems. Educators must understand how bias can be inadvertently introduced into algorithms and learn strategies for mitigating it within the classroom setting. They should also be knowledgeable about the ethical implications of AI technology use and be able to guide students through discussions on responsible development and deployment of these systems.

Overcoming Bias and Stereotypes in AI Education

Overcoming bias and stereotypes in AI education requires a comprehensive understanding of the ways in which these biases can manifest within algorithms and a commitment to implementing strategies that mitigate their impact. When it comes to AI education, addressing bias and stereotypes is crucial for creating an inclusive learning environment that fosters belonging. Here are three key points to consider:

- Awareness: Educators must be aware of the potential biases embedded in AI algorithms and how they can perpetuate stereotypes. This awareness allows them to critically evaluate educational materials, tools, and resources before incorporating them into the curriculum.
- Curriculum Design: Developing an inclusive curriculum is essential for overcoming bias and stereotypes in AI education. It should promote diversity, represent different perspectives, and challenge existing biases. This involves ensuring that all students have access to diverse role models within the field of AI.
- Ethical Considerations: Educators must prioritize ethical considerations when teaching AI concepts. This includes discussing the potential societal impacts of

biased algorithms and promoting responsible use of technology. By instilling ethical principles early on, students will develop a sense of responsibility towards creating unbiased AI systems.

Empowering Black Children in AI Education

Empowering underrepresented students in AI education requires a deliberate focus on creating an inclusive learning environment that recognizes and addresses the unique barriers they may face. In the case of black children, there are several challenges that need to be addressed to ensure their empowerment in AI education.

One key challenge is access to resources. Black children often have limited access to technology and internet connectivity at home, which can hinder their ability to engage with AI learning materials. Schools and educational institutions must work towards providing equal access to these resources, whether by offering technological infrastructure or facilitating access through community centers or libraries.

Another challenge lies in teacher training. It is crucial for educators to receive adequate training on AI concepts and methods so that they can effectively teach black children. This includes understanding potential biases within AI algorithms and how they may disproportionately affect marginalized communities. By equipping teachers with the necessary knowledge and skills, we can ensure that black children receive high-quality instruction in AI education.

Furthermore, fostering a sense of belonging is essential for empowering black children in AI education. Creating a supportive classroom environment where students feel valued, respected, and included can enhance their motivation and engagement with the subject matter. Teachers should actively promote diversity and multiculturalism within the classroom while addressing any instances of bias or discrimination that may arise.

Frequently Asked Questions

How Can the Limited Access to AI Resources Be Addressed Specifically for Black Children?

The limited access to AI resources for black children can be addressed through targeted interventions that focus on providing equitable access to technological resources, ensuring culturally responsive curriculum, and offering comprehensive teacher training programs.

What Are Some Strategies to Bridge the Digital Divide in AI Education for Black Children?

Strategies to bridge the digital divide in AI education for black children include ensuring equitable access to resources, providing comprehensive teacher training, promoting community partnerships, implementing culturally responsive pedagogy, and addressing systemic barriers.

What Is the Significance of Teacher Training in AI Education for Black Children?

Teacher training in AI education for black children is significant as it equips educators with the necessary skills and knowledge to effectively teach AI concepts. This ensures that students receive quality instruction and are prepared for future opportunities in this field.

How Can Bias and Stereotypes Be Effectively Addressed in AI Education for Black Children?

Bias and stereotypes in AI education for black children can be effectively addressed through the implementation of inclusive curriculum, diverse representation in educational materials, promoting critical thinking skills, and providing ongoing professional development for teachers.

What Are Some Ways to Empower Black Children in AI Education and Ensure Their Equal Opportunities in the Field?

To empower black children in AI education and ensure equal opportunities, strategies may include promoting inclusive curricula, providing equitable access to resources, fostering a supportive learning environment, and offering comprehensive teacher training programs.

Conclusion

In conclusion, addressing the challenges in AI education for black children requires a multi-faceted approach. It is crucial to ensure access to AI resources and bridge the digital divide to provide equal opportunities for learning.

Teacher training plays a vital role in equipping educators with the necessary knowledge and skills to effectively teach AI concepts.

Additionally, overcoming bias and stereotypes in AI education is essential for fostering inclusivity.

By empowering black children in AI education, we can create a more diverse and equitable future.

One interesting statistic shows that only 5% of high school students have access to computer science courses that include AI or machine learning components (Code.org).

Solutions for Overcoming Challenges through Collaboration and Black Community Involvement in AI Education for Black Children

What are the key factors that contribute to overcoming challenges in AI education for black children?

This section examines the importance of collaboration and black community involvement in addressing these challenges. By leveraging partnerships and innovative approaches, this research aims to provide solutions that empower black children through AI education.

Furthermore, it explores how addressing equity and access can enhance the effectiveness of AI education initiatives for this demographic. Ultimately, this study seeks to foster a sense of belonging by engaging an audience interested in promoting inclusivity in educational settings.

Key Takeaways

- Collaboration and community involvement in AI education for black children enhance learning outcomes and promote a more inclusive and equitable educational environment.
- Building partnerships with local organizations and institutions can pool resources and expertise, facilitate workshops and training sessions, and expose black children to real-world applications of AI technology.
- Addressing equity and access in AI education for black children involves developing culturally responsive curricula, providing professional development programs for educators, and offering resources, mentorship programs, and extracurricular activities.
- Fostering curiosity, inclusion, and empowerment in AI education for black children requires encouraging natural curiosity, creating safe spaces, pairing them with experienced mentors, and equipping them with valuable AI skills through resources and opportunities.

The Importance of Collaboration in AI Education for Black Children

The significance of collaboration in the context of AI education for black children can be observed through its potential to enhance learning outcomes and promote a more inclusive and equitable educational environment. Collaboration refers to the process of individuals or groups working together towards a common goal, sharing ideas, resources, and expertise.

In the field of AI education, collaboration plays a crucial role in fostering creativity, critical thinking skills, and problem-solving abilities among black children. Collaboration allows for diverse perspectives to be considered, leading to a richer understanding of concepts and ideas. When black children collaborate with their peers or educators in AI education settings, they are exposed to different ways of thinking and approaching problems. This exposure not only broadens their knowledge base but also helps them develop empathy and appreciation for different viewpoints.

Furthermore, collaboration promotes an inclusive educational environment by breaking down barriers between individuals. By working together on projects or tasks related to AI education, black children have the opportunity to interact with others who may come from different cultural backgrounds or have varying levels of expertise. This interaction fosters mutual respect and understanding while creating an environment where all voices are valued.

Leveraging Black Community Involvement to Overcome Challenges in AI Education

To address the obstacles in AI education, leveraging the active participation of the black community proves essential. Involving the black community can help overcome challenges and create a sense of belonging for black children in AI education.

Here are three ways in which black community involvement can be leveraged:

- Mentorship programs: Establishing mentorship programs within the black community can provide guidance and support to black children interested in AI education. Mentors from similar backgrounds can serve as role models, offering advice on educational pathways, career opportunities, and personal growth.
- Community partnerships: Collaborating with local organizations and institutions within the black community can enhance access to resources and opportunities for AI education. By forming partnerships with schools, nonprofits, and businesses, initiatives can be developed that cater specifically to the needs of black children.
- Representation in curriculum: Including diverse perspectives within AI curricula is crucial for fostering a sense of belonging among black students. Incorporating examples and case studies that highlight contributions made by individuals from the black community not only promotes cultural inclusion but also inspires young learners.

Building Partnerships for Success in AI Education for Black Children

Establishing partnerships with local organizations and institutions can enhance access to resources and opportunities, promoting success in AI education for black children. Collaborative efforts between educational institutions, community organizations, and industry stakeholders can provide a comprehensive approach to addressing the challenges faced by black children in AI education. By working together, these partnerships can ensure that black children have equal access to quality AI education programs.

Building partnerships with local organizations allows for the pooling of resources and expertise. Community-based organizations can offer valuable insights into the specific needs of black children in their communities, ensuring that educational programs are tailored to address these needs effectively. Additionally, partnerships with industry stakeholders can expose black children to real-world applications of AI technology through internships, mentorship programs, or field trips.

Institutions such as schools and universities play a crucial role in fostering collaboration. They can facilitate partnerships by providing space for workshops, seminars, or training sessions focused on AI education for black children. Moreover, they can establish relationships with external organizations to secure funding or sponsorships for initiatives aimed at enhancing access to AI resources.

Addressing Equity and Access in AI Education for Black Children

Addressing equity and access in AI education requires a comprehensive approach that involves collaboration between educational institutions, community organizations, and industry stakeholders. This ensures that all black children have equal opportunities to engage with and benefit from AI education.

To create an inclusive and equitable AI education system for black children, the following steps can be taken:

- **Curriculum Development**: Develop culturally responsive curricula that incorporate diverse perspectives and experiences of black communities. This will foster a sense of belonging among black students and promote their engagement in AI education.
- **Teacher Training**: Provide professional development programs for educators on culturally relevant pedagogy and effective instruction strategies for teaching AI concepts to black children. This will enhance teachers' ability to create inclusive learning environments.
- **Community Engagement**: Establish partnerships with community organizations to provide resources, mentorship programs, and extracurricular activities related to AI education for black children. This collaboration will ensure that students have access to additional support outside of the classroom.

Innovative Approaches to Black Community Engagement in AI Education

Innovative approaches to fostering engagement with AI education within the black community can contribute to a more inclusive and equitable learning environment. By actively involving the black community in AI education, barriers to access and equity can be addressed effectively.

One such approach is the establishment of community-based AI education programs that are tailored specifically for black students. These programs provide a platform for students to explore AI concepts, develop technical skills, and engage in hands-on projects. In addition, partnerships between educational institutions and community organizations can facilitate the integration of AI education into existing curricula.

Furthermore, mentorship programs play a crucial role in engaging black students in AI education. Pairing black students with mentors who have expertise in AI not only provides guidance but also fosters a sense of belonging within the field. Additionally, hosting workshops and conferences focused on AI education within the black community creates opportunities for networking and collaboration among students, educators, researchers, and industry professionals.

Engagement with AI education within the black community should also emphasize cultural relevance by incorporating examples and case studies that resonate with black experiences. This approach ensures that learners feel seen and validated while promoting a deeper understanding of how AI impacts diverse communities.

Overall, innovative approaches that prioritize engagement with AI education within the black community are essential for creating an inclusive learning environment where all individuals feel valued and supported on their educational journey.

Empowering Black Children through AI Education and Collaboration

A key aspect of fostering empowerment among black children in the realm of AI is by creating opportunities for them to actively participate and collaborate in AI-related projects. Engaging black children in AI education and collaboration not only equips them with valuable skills but also helps to build a sense of belonging and community.

In order to achieve this, several approaches can be implemented:

- Cultivating curiosity: Encouraging black children's natural curiosity about AI technology can spark their interest and motivate them to explore further.

- Providing inclusive learning environments: Creating safe spaces where black children feel supported and included allows them to express themselves freely and engage actively in AI education.
- Promoting mentorship programs: Pairing black children with mentors who are experienced in AI can provide guidance, encouragement, and support throughout their learning journey.

By implementing these approaches, we can foster empowerment among black children in the field of AI by providing them with opportunities for active participation, creating an inclusive environment that promotes a sense of belonging, and facilitating mentorship relationships that inspire growth.

This collaborative approach ensures that black children have the resources they need to thrive in the world of artificial intelligence.

Frequently Asked Questions

How Does Collaboration in AI Education Benefit Black Children Specifically?

Collaboration in AI education benefits black children specifically by creating an inclusive learning environment that addresses their unique needs, promotes diversity and representation in the field, and fosters a sense of empowerment and belonging.

What Are Some Specific Challenges That Black Communities Face in AI Education?

Challenges faced by black communities in AI education include limited access to resources, lack of representation and diversity in the field, systemic barriers, and unconscious bias. These challenges hinder equitable opportunities for black children to engage in AI education.

How Can the Black Community Be More Involved in AI Education Initiatives?

To increase black community involvement in AI education initiatives, strategies such as enhancing access to resources, promoting mentorship programs, fostering partnerships with educational institutions, and creating culturally relevant curriculum can be implemented.

What Are Some Successful Partnerships That Have Been Formed to Improve AI Education for Black Children?

Successful partnerships have been formed to improve AI education for black children. These collaborations involve various stakeholders such as educational institutions, tech companies, and community organizations, working together to provide resources, mentorship, and opportunities for black students in the field of AI.

What Are Some Innovative Approaches That Have Been Used to Engage the Black Community in AI Education?

Innovative approaches used to engage the black community in AI education include creating culturally relevant curriculum, partnering with community organizations, hosting workshops and events, providing mentorship programs, and utilizing social media platforms for outreach and information dissemination.

Conclusion

In conclusion, collaboration and black community involvement play crucial roles in overcoming challenges in AI education for black children. By leveraging partnerships and innovative approaches, we can address issues of equity and access in this field.

Empowering black children through AI education not only benefits their individual growth but also contributes to the overall diversification of talent in the AI industry. According to a study by Code.org, only 14% of computer science graduates are African Americans, highlighting the need for increased efforts in providing opportunities for black students in AI education.

The Potential Long-Term Impact of a Generation of AI-Literate Black Individuals

In an era characterized by rapid advancements in artificial intelligence (AI), the emergence of a generation of AI-literate black individuals stands as a significant development.

This phenomenon holds potential implications that could shape the future and break barriers, ultimately resulting in long-term impact within the black community.

By empowering individuals with AI literacy, this transformative movement has the capacity to shift their roles from mere consumers to creators, fostering a sense of belonging and ownership within the wider technological landscape.

Key Takeaways

- Increased diversity and representation in the AI community, driven by efforts to promote inclusivity, can lead to the development of unbiased and ethical AI systems.
- AI-literate Black individuals can bring diverse perspectives and experiences to AI algorithm and system development, addressing biases and inequalities that arise from homogeneous teams.
- In healthcare, AI-literate Black individuals can contribute to improving diagnostic accuracy, reducing health disparities, and enhancing access to quality healthcare through the effective use of AI tools.
- AI-literate Black individuals can play a significant role in finance and education by using AI applications to navigate complex datasets, address disparities, empower individuals to make informed decisions, and enhance educational opportunities and outcomes for underrepresented communities.

The Rise of AI-Literate Black Individuals

The increasing prevalence of AI-literate black individuals indicates a growing trend towards greater technological literacy and opportunities for inclusion in the field of artificial intelligence. This rise can be attributed to several factors, including increased access to education and training programs, as well as efforts to promote diversity and representation within the AI community.

One key driver behind this trend is the recognition that diverse perspectives are essential for the development of unbiased and ethical AI systems. Research has shown that AI algorithms often reflect biases present in their training data, leading to discriminatory outcomes. By including more black individuals in the design and development process, there is a greater potential for creating fairer and more inclusive technologies.

Moreover, initiatives such as coding boot camps, scholarships, and mentorship programs have emerged to provide opportunities for underrepresented groups, including black individuals, to gain skills in AI-related fields. These programs aim to bridge the digital divide by providing resources and support necessary for success in an increasingly tech-driven society.

Overall, the rise of AI-literate black individuals signifies progress towards a more inclusive future. It not only empowers marginalized communities but also contributes to addressing systemic biases within AI technology. By fostering belongingness through education and equal access to opportunities, we can harness the full potential of diverse talent in shaping a more equitable AI landscape.

Shaping the Future: How AI-Literate Black Individuals Can Make a Difference

Shaping the future involves exploring how individuals with knowledge and understanding of AI can contribute to societal advancements. In the context of AI-literate black individuals, their potential long-term impact can be significant. By embracing AI literacy, these individuals can actively participate in various sectors such as technology, healthcare, finance, and education.

In the technology sector, AI-literate black individuals can bring diverse perspectives and experiences that enrich the development of AI algorithms and systems. Their involvement can help address biases and inequalities that may arise from homogeneous teams designing AI technologies. This inclusivity promotes fairness and equity in algorithmic decision-making processes.

AI-literate black individuals can also make a difference in healthcare by leveraging their knowledge to improve diagnostic accuracy, treatment plans, and personalized medicine. By utilizing AI tools effectively, they can contribute to reducing health disparities within marginalized communities.

Furthermore, in finance and education sectors, their expertise in AI enables them to navigate complex datasets for more informed decision-making. This empowers them to create innovative solutions that cater specifically to the needs of underrepresented communities.

Overall, the active participation of AI-literate black individuals has the potential to foster social progress by ensuring diversity and inclusion within AI development processes across various domains.

Breaking Barriers: Unleashing the Potential of AI-Literate Black Individuals

Breaking barriers for AI-literate individuals from the black community involves unlocking their full potential and creating opportunities for meaningful contributions in various sectors. The advancement of artificial intelligence (AI) has transformed the way we live, work, and interact with technology. However, access to AI education and opportunities remains unequal across different communities. Addressing this disparity is crucial not only for social justice but also for fostering innovation and inclusivity.

To enable AI-literate individuals from the black community to thrive, it is essential to provide them with comprehensive education and training programs that encompass both technical skills and critical thinking abilities. These programs should be accessible, affordable, and culturally sensitive to cater to the unique needs of this community. Additionally, mentorship initiatives can play a significant role in guiding aspiring AI professionals towards successful careers by providing guidance, support, and networking opportunities.

Creating inclusive spaces within the tech industry is another important factor in breaking barriers for AI-literate individuals from the black community. Companies need to actively promote diversity through inclusive hiring practices, diverse leadership representation, and equitable compensation structures. Furthermore, establishing partnerships between educational institutions and industry leaders can facilitate internships and job placements for aspiring AI professionals.

Empowering the Community: The Long-Term Impact of AI Literacy for Black Individuals

Empowering the community through AI literacy has the potential to create lasting positive effects on the social and economic well-being of individuals from marginalized backgrounds. By equipping black individuals with AI skills, they can actively participate in the increasingly digital world and contribute to its development. The long-term impact of AI literacy for black individuals extends beyond personal growth; it also benefits their communities as a whole.

AI literacy provides black individuals with opportunities to break free from traditional barriers that have hindered their progress. Increased access to education and training in AI empowers them to develop innovative solutions and address challenges specific to their communities. This not only fosters self-reliance but also nurtures a sense of belonging within these communities.

Furthermore, an AI-literate generation of black individuals contributes significantly to closing racial gaps in employment and income inequality. With AI becoming integral across various industries, acquiring these skills enhances employability prospects for marginalized populations. This leads to increased financial stability, improved job satisfaction, and reduced poverty rates among black communities.

The long-term impact of empowering the community through AI literacy is multifaceted. It promotes social cohesion, as diverse voices are included in shaping technological advancements that reflect the needs of all members of society. Additionally, by fostering economic empowerment, AI literacy creates pathways for upward mobility and ultimately bridges socioeconomic disparities among marginalized groups.

From Consumers to Creators: How AI Literacy Is Transforming the Black Community

The transformation of the black community through AI literacy is evident as individuals transition from being consumers to creators, actively participating in the development and application of artificial intelligence technologies. This shift towards becoming active contributors within the realm of AI has significant implications for the long-term impact on the black community.

By acquiring AI literacy skills, black individuals not only gain access to opportunities within various sectors but also contribute to shaping the future of technology. As creators, they can address existing biases and disparities in AI systems that may disproportionately affect marginalized communities. Additionally, their participation in developing AI technologies ensures a more inclusive representation of perspectives and experiences.

Furthermore, this transition from consumers to creators empowers black individuals by fostering a sense of agency and ownership. It enables them to challenge dominant narratives and redefine their roles as both beneficiaries and architects of technological advancements. By actively engaging with AI tools and platforms, they can shape solutions that cater specifically to their own needs and aspirations.

Frequently Asked Questions

How Can AI Literacy Benefit the Broader Black Community Beyond Individual Empowerment?

The potential long-term impact of a generation of AI-literate Black individuals extends beyond individual empowerment, benefiting the broader Black community. AI literacy can lead to increased access to opportunities, reduced disparities, and enhanced socio-economic outcomes for the community as a whole.

What Are Some Potential Challenges or Barriers That AI-Literate Black Individuals Might Face in Their Pursuit of Making a Difference?

Potential challenges and barriers may arise for AI-literate Black individuals seeking to effect change. These could include systemic racism, limited access to resources, biased algorithms, and lack of representation in decision-making processes.

Are There Any Specific Industries or Fields Where the Impact of AI-Literate Black Individuals Is Expected to Be Particularly Significant?

The potential long-term impact of a generation of AI-literate black individuals is expected to be particularly significant in industries or fields that rely heavily on technology and data analysis, such as finance, healthcare, transportation, and telecommunications.

How Can AI Literacy Contribute to Addressing Systemic Inequalities and Promoting Social Justice Within the Black Community?

The potential long-term impact of a generation of AI-literate black individuals on addressing systemic inequalities and promoting social justice within the black community lies in their ability to leverage AI technologies for equitable opportunities and inclusive decision-making processes.

What Are Some Examples of Successful Initiatives or Programs That Have Already Fostered AI Literacy Among Black Individuals, and What Lessons Can Be Learned from Them?

Successful initiatives and programs fostering AI literacy among Black individuals include organizations like Black in AI and AI4ALL. These initiatives provide educational resources, mentorship, and networking opportunities to promote inclusivity and diversity in the field of AI.

Conclusion

In conclusion, the emergence of a generation of AI-literate black individuals has the potential to bring about significant long-term impact. By gaining knowledge and skills in artificial intelligence, these individuals can contribute to shaping the future, breaking barriers, and empowering their community.

Just as a single drop of water can create ripples that extend far beyond its initial impact, the influence of AI literacy within the black community will spread and transform it from mere consumers into creators. This transformative power has the capacity to revolutionize not only individual lives but also society as a whole.

JOHN ANGUS SCANTLING JR

A Vision for a More Inclusive and Technologically Empowered Future

In the pursuit of a more inclusive and technologically empowered future, the role of technology in promoting inclusivity has garnered significant attention.

This section aims to explore how technological advancements can create equal opportunities for all individuals, particularly those from marginalized communities.

By examining the barriers to inclusion in the digital age, this section seeks to envision a future characterized by digital equality and technological empowerment.

Through an objective and impersonal analysis, this section will shed light on the potential transformative impact of technology in fostering belonging and societal progress.

Key Takeaways

- Eliminating barriers to access such as limited internet connectivity and affordable devices.
- Providing equal opportunities for marginalized communities to acquire digital skills.
- Fostering diversity within tech companies to address unique needs.
- Promoting multilingual content for effective communication.

The Role of Technology in Promoting Inclusivity

Technology plays a pivotal role in fostering inclusivity by providing equal opportunities and access to resources for individuals from diverse backgrounds. In today's interconnected world, technology has become an essential tool in creating a more inclusive society. It breaks down barriers of distance, time, and physical limitations, enabling people from different cultural, social, and economic backgrounds to connect and interact with one another.

One way technology promotes inclusivity is through improved access to information and education. The internet serves as a vast repository of knowledge that can be accessed by anyone with an internet connection. This allows individuals from marginalized communities or remote areas to acquire the same educational resources as those in more privileged settings. Online courses and digital libraries provide opportunities for lifelong learning, empowering individuals to enhance their skills and knowledge regardless of their background.

Furthermore, technology facilitates communication across geographical boundaries. Social media platforms enable people to share ideas, experiences, and perspectives instantaneously with others around the world. This exchange of information fosters understanding, empathy, and mutual respect among diverse groups.

Additionally, assistive technologies have revolutionized the lives of individuals with disabilities by providing them with greater independence and accessibility. Innovations such as screen readers for visually impaired individuals or voice recognition software for those with mobility impairments enable them to engage fully in various aspects of life like education or employment.

Creating Equal Opportunities through Technological Advancements

The creation of equal opportunities can be facilitated through the advancement of technological tools and systems. Technology has the potential to break down barriers and provide access to resources, information, and opportunities that were once limited or unavailable.

Here are five ways in which technological advancements can contribute to creating equal opportunities:

- **Digital platforms**: Online platforms have opened up new avenues for education, employment, and entrepreneurship, allowing individuals from diverse backgrounds to access opportunities regardless of their geographical location.
- **Artificial intelligence (AI)**: AI technologies can help reduce bias in decision-making processes by removing human prejudices. This can lead to fairer outcomes in areas such as hiring practices or loan approvals.
- **Assistive technologies**: Technological innovations like screen readers or braille displays enable individuals with disabilities to participate fully in educational and professional settings by providing them with tools for communication, learning, and productivity.
- **Mobile technology**: The widespread availability of mobile devices has enabled marginalized communities to access essential services such as healthcare, banking, and e-commerce conveniently and affordably.
- **Data-driven policies**: The use of data analytics allows policymakers to identify disparities in various sectors such as education or healthcare. By understanding these gaps, targeted interventions can be designed to address inequalities effectively.

Empowering Marginalized Communities with Technological Solutions

Empowering marginalized communities through the utilization of technological solutions can help bridge the gap between them and mainstream society. Technological advancements have the potential to provide marginalized communities with access to resources, opportunities, and platforms that were previously inaccessible. By leveraging technology, these communities can gain a voice and participate actively in societal discussions.

For instance, social media platforms offer an avenue for individuals from marginalized backgrounds to share their experiences, express their opinions, and connect with others who may face similar challenges. This not only fosters a sense of belonging but also allows for the formation of supportive networks.

Moreover, technological solutions can address existing disparities by providing equal access to education and employment opportunities. Online learning platforms enable individuals from marginalized communities to acquire new skills and knowledge without being limited by geographical or financial constraints. Similarly, remote work options facilitated by technology allow individuals to overcome barriers such as transportation issues or discrimination in traditional workplace settings.

Overcoming Barriers to Inclusion in the Digital Age

Addressing barriers to inclusion in the digital age requires a comprehensive understanding of the challenges faced by marginalized communities in accessing and utilizing technological resources. In order to create a more inclusive and technologically empowered future, it is crucial to identify and overcome these barriers.

- Limited access to technology: Many marginalized communities lack access to affordable and reliable internet connectivity, devices, and infrastructure necessary for digital participation.

- Digital literacy gaps: Unequal opportunities for education and training result in limited digital literacy skills, hindering marginalized individuals from fully participating in the digital world.
- Language and cultural barriers: Language differences can make it difficult for individuals from diverse backgrounds to navigate online platforms or access information effectively.
- Discrimination and bias: Online spaces often perpetuate biases against marginalized groups, leading to exclusionary practices that further alienate these communities.
- Lack of representation: The underrepresentation of marginalized communities in the development of technological solutions results in products that do not adequately address their unique needs.

To promote inclusivity, stakeholders must collaborate to address these barriers. This can involve initiatives such as providing affordable internet access, offering digital literacy programs tailored to the specific needs of marginalized communities, fostering diversity within tech companies, promoting multilingual content, combating online discrimination through policy changes, and encouraging active participation from all segments of society.

Envisioning a Future of Digital Equality and Technological Empowerment

To achieve digital equality and foster technological empowerment, it is essential to envision a future where marginalized communities have equal access to and opportunities for utilizing digital resources. This vision entails creating an inclusive and technologically empowered society where all individuals, regardless of their socioeconomic background or cultural identity, can fully participate in the digital age.

In this envisioned future, barriers to access such as limited internet connectivity and lack of affordable devices would be eliminated. Marginalized communities would have equal opportunities to acquire the necessary skills and knowledge needed to navigate the digital landscape. Educational institutions and community organizations would play a crucial role in providing training programs tailored to the specific needs of these communities.

Furthermore, policies would be enacted to ensure that technology companies prioritize inclusivity in product design and development. This includes considering diverse perspectives during the creation process and actively seeking feedback from underrepresented groups.

By embracing diversity and fostering a sense of belonging within the digital realm, marginalized communities will not only gain access to educational resources but also have greater agency over their own narratives. With increased representation in online spaces, these communities will be able to challenge stereotypes and create more accurate portrayals of their experiences.

Ultimately, by envisioning a future where everyone has equal access to digital resources and opportunities for technological empowerment, we can work towards building a more inclusive society that values diversity and ensures that no one is left behind in the rapidly advancing digital age.

Frequently Asked Questions

How Can Technology Be Leveraged to Promote Inclusivity in Education and Healthcare?

Technology can be leveraged to promote inclusivity in education and healthcare through the provision of accessible and personalized learning platforms, telemedicine services, and remote monitoring tools, ultimately ensuring equal access to quality education and healthcare for all individuals.

What Are Some Examples of Technological Advancements That Have Helped Create Equal Opportunities for Marginalized Communities?

Technological advancements have contributed to equal opportunities for marginalized communities. For instance, the development of online educational platforms has provided access to quality education for individuals who were previously hindered by geographical or economic constraints. Similarly, telemedicine has enabled remote healthcare services, benefiting those in underserved areas.

How Can Technological Solutions Empower Individuals with Disabilities to Actively Participate in Society?

Technological solutions can empower individuals with disabilities to actively participate in society by providing assistive devices, communication tools, and accessibility features. These advancements can enhance their mobility, communication, and access to information, fostering inclusivity and enabling greater societal engagement.

What Are the Biggest Challenges Faced by Marginalized Communities in Accessing and Utilizing Technology?

The biggest challenges faced by marginalized communities in accessing and utilizing technology include limited access to infrastructure, lack of digital literacy skills, affordability issues, and systemic barriers. Overcoming these obstacles is crucial for a more inclusive and technologically empowered future.

How Can a Future of Digital Equality and Technological Empowerment Be Achieved on a Global Scale?

Achieving a future of global digital equality and technological empowerment requires addressing the challenges faced by marginalized communities in accessing and utilizing technology. This can be accomplished through inclusive policies, improved infrastructure, and targeted education and training programs.

Conclusion

In conclusion, technology plays a crucial role in promoting inclusivity by creating equal opportunities and empowering marginalized communities. By overcoming barriers to inclusion in the digital age, we can envision a future of digital equality and technological empowerment for all.

One interesting statistic to consider is that according to a study conducted by the World Bank, increasing internet access by 10% can boost a country's GDP by an average of 1.38%. This highlights the immense potential of technology in driving economic growth and reducing inequalities globally.

CONCLUSION

Key Points Discussed Throughout the Book Regarding AI Education for Black Children

This section aims to summarize the key points discussed throughout the book regarding AI education for black children.

The importance of AI education for this specific demographic is highlighted, given the existing disparities in access and resources.

Strategies to enhance AI education are explored, with a focus on promoting diversity and inclusion in order to empower black children through their engagement with AI technologies.

By addressing these issues, this section contributes to the ongoing dialogue on equity and inclusivity in educational settings.

Key Takeaways

- AI education for black children ensures equitable access to opportunities and resources.
- It empowers black children to navigate and thrive in a technology-driven society.
- Addressing disparities in AI education requires a comprehensive approach, including access to resources, culturally relevant curriculum, and equitable learning environments.
- Promoting diversity and inclusion in AI education for black children is essential, through incorporating diverse perspectives, integrating culturally relevant content, and establishing inclusive classroom norms and mentorship programs.

The Importance of AI Education for Black Children

The significance of providing AI education to black children has been emphasized throughout the book. AI education plays a crucial role in ensuring that black children have equitable access to opportunities and resources in an increasingly digital world. By offering AI education, we empower black children with the knowledge and skills necessary to navigate and thrive in a technology-driven society.

AI education for black children is important for several reasons. Firstly, it addresses the existing racial disparities in access to technological education. Historically, black communities have faced systemic barriers that limit their educational opportunities, resulting in a lack of representation and inclusion in technology-related fields. By providing AI education specifically targeting black children, we can bridge this gap and promote inclusivity.

Secondly, AI education equips black children with the tools they need to actively participate in shaping the future of technology. As AI becomes more prevalent across various industries, it is essential that all communities are represented in its development and decision-making processes.

Without adequate AI education, black children risk being left behind or limited to passive consumers rather than active creators and innovators.

Addressing the Disparities in AI Education for Black Children

Addressing the disparities in AI education for black children requires a comprehensive approach that considers factors such as access to resources, culturally relevant curriculum, and equitable learning environments.

In order to bridge the gap in AI education, it is vital to ensure that all students, regardless of their racial or ethnic background, have equal opportunities to engage with this subject. One key aspect of addressing these disparities is providing access to resources such as computers, software, and internet connectivity. This allows black children to fully participate in AI education and develop the necessary skills for success in this field.

Another important factor to consider is the development of culturally relevant curriculum. It is crucial that AI education materials reflect the experiences and perspectives of black children. This can help foster a sense of belonging and relevance within the learning environment. Additionally, an equitable learning environment must be established where black children have equal access to quality teachers and educational opportunities.

Furthermore, it is essential to address any biases or stereotypes present within AI technology itself. By promoting diversity and inclusivity in AI development processes, we can ensure that technologies are fair and unbiased when applied across different racial and ethnic groups.

Strategies to Enhance AI Education for Black Children

Strategies for enhancing AI education for black children encompass various approaches that aim to promote equal access, cultural relevance, and equitable learning environments.

One such strategy is the expansion of STEM programs in schools serving predominantly black communities. These programs provide opportunities for students to engage with AI technologies and develop their skills in this field.

Additionally, partnerships between educational institutions and industry professionals can help expose black children to real-world applications of AI and provide mentorship opportunities.

Another strategy involves incorporating culturally relevant content into AI education curricula. This approach recognizes the importance of representation and allows black children to see themselves reflected in the materials they study. It also helps foster a sense of belonging and promotes engagement with the subject matter.

Furthermore, creating inclusive learning environments is crucial for enhancing AI education for black children. This involves implementing anti-bias training for educators, ensuring diverse voices are represented in classroom discussions, and providing resources that address racial disparities within the field of AI.

Promoting Diversity and Inclusion in AI Education for Black Children

Promoting diversity and inclusion in AI education for black children requires a multifaceted approach that encompasses curriculum development, teacher training, and the creation of supportive learning environments. To achieve these goals, several strategies can be implemented:

Curriculum Development:

- Incorporate diverse perspectives and examples in AI education materials.
- Include topics related to ethics, bias, and social implications of AI technologies.
- Integrate culturally relevant content that reflects the experiences of black children.

Teacher Training:

- Provide professional development opportunities on culturally responsive teaching practices.
- Offer training on incorporating AI education into existing curricula.
- Foster awareness about unconscious biases in teaching practices and provide strategies to mitigate them.

Supportive Learning Environments:

- Establish inclusive classroom norms that value diversity and respect different perspectives.
- Create mentorship programs connecting black students with professionals working in AI fields.
- Foster collaboration among students from diverse backgrounds to promote understanding and empathy.

Empowering Black Children through AI Education

Empowering black children through AI education involves providing them with the necessary knowledge and skills to engage in the field of artificial intelligence, thereby fostering their intellectual growth and future opportunities. By equipping black children with AI education, they are given a platform for learning and developing critical thinking abilities. This allows them to actively participate in an increasingly technological society and contribute to advancements in AI research.

AI education for black children also serves as a means of bridging the racial gap within the field. Historically, there has been underrepresentation of Black individuals in STEM fields, including AI. By offering AI education specifically targeted towards black children, it aims to create a more inclusive environment where everyone feels empowered to pursue their interests and talents.

Furthermore, empowering black children through AI education can lead to increased diversity within the field. Diversity is crucial as it brings different perspectives, experiences, and ideas into the development of AI technologies. It fosters innovation by challenging existing biases and promoting fairness in algorithmic decision-making processes.

Frequently Asked Questions

What Are the Specific Challenges Faced by Black Children in Accessing AI Education?

The specific challenges faced by black children in accessing AI education include limited access to resources, lack of representation and role models, implicit bias in educational systems, and systemic inequalities that perpetuate disparities in educational opportunities.

How Can Parents and Communities Support and Encourage Black Children in Pursuing AI Education?

Parents and communities play a crucial role in supporting and encouraging black children to pursue AI education. By providing resources, mentorship, and creating inclusive environments, they can empower these children to overcome challenges and excel in this field.

Are There Any Existing Initiatives or Programs That Focus on AI Education for Black Children?

Existing initiatives and programs that focus on AI education for black children are discussed in the book. These initiatives aim to provide equal opportunities, promote diversity, and empower black students to excel in the field of AI.

What Are the Potential Long-Term Benefits of Providing AI Education to Black Children?

The potential long-term benefits of providing AI education to black children include empowering them with the knowledge and skills necessary to navigate an increasingly technology-driven world, promoting diversity in the field, and addressing historical disparities in access to educational opportunities.

How Can Policymakers and Educational Institutions Collaborate to Ensure Equal Opportunities for Black Children in AI Education?

To ensure equal opportunities for black children in AI education, policymakers and educational institutions must collaborate. This collaboration can involve implementing inclusive curricula, providing resources and support, and addressing systemic barriers that hinder access to AI education.

Conclusion

In conclusion, the book highlights the significance of AI education for black children and emphasizes the need to address disparities in this field.

Strategies to enhance AI education are discussed, including promoting diversity and inclusion to empower black children.

By equipping them with AI knowledge and skills, we can ensure their active participation in shaping the future of technology.

One interesting statistic mentioned is that only 5% of employees in major tech companies are African American, underscoring the importance of providing equal opportunities for black children in AI education.

Reinforce the Importance of Early AI Education for Black Children's Development

In the realm of education, the significance of early AI education for black children's development stands as a foundational pillar. This section aims to underscore the benefits of introducing AI education at an early stage in the lives of black children, exploring its potential to enhance their cognitive skills and stimulate creativity.

Additionally, this section will address how early AI education can help bridge the opportunity gap that disproportionately affects black children, ultimately empowering them on their educational journey.

By emphasizing these aspects, we hope to provide a visual representation of the importance and transformative potential of early AI education for black children's development.

Key Takeaways
- Early AI education for black children can enhance their cognitive skills and problem-solving abilities.

- It can provide increased opportunities for future career advancement and development of critical thinking skills.
- Early AI education can also enhance black children's creativity by introducing new technologies and encouraging exploration of different ways of thinking.
- To reinforce the importance of early AI education for black children's development, it is crucial to address the opportunity gap through culturally responsive curriculum, qualified educators, necessary technological infrastructure, collaboration, and mentorship programs.

The Benefits of Early AI Education for Black Children

The benefits of early AI education for black children include enhanced cognitive skills, improved problem-solving abilities, and increased opportunities for future career advancement.

Early exposure to AI education can have a positive impact on the cognitive development of black children. By learning about artificial intelligence and its applications at a young age, children are exposed to complex concepts that stimulate their critical thinking skills and improve their ability to analyze information. This early exposure also enhances their problem-solving abilities as they learn how to use AI tools and algorithms to tackle various challenges.

Moreover, early AI education provides black children with increased opportunities for future career advancement. In today's technologically driven world, proficiency in AI is becoming increasingly valuable in many industries. By introducing AI education at an early stage, black children are given a head start in developing the necessary skills and knowledge required for careers in fields such as data science, machine learning, robotics, and computer programming.

Additionally, early AI education helps foster a sense of belonging among black children. By providing them with equal access to educational resources and opportunities related to AI, it sends a powerful message that their talents and potential are recognized and valued. This sense of belonging can contribute to higher levels of self-esteem and motivation among black children as they see themselves represented in the field of technology.

How Early AI Education Can Enhance Black Children's Cognitive Skills

Enhancing the cognitive skills of black children can be achieved through early exposure to AI education. Research has shown that early AI education provides numerous benefits for the cognitive development of black children. By engaging with AI technologies from a young age, black children have the opportunity to develop critical thinking skills, problem-solving abilities, and creativity. These cognitive skills are essential for academic success and future career opportunities.

Early exposure to AI education allows black children to explore new concepts and ideas in a supportive and inclusive environment. This fosters a sense of belonging and encourages active participation in learning activities. Moreover, AI education provides opportunities for black children to engage in collaborative projects, promoting teamwork and social interaction.

Furthermore, AI education helps improve memory retention and enhances information processing skills among black children. Through interactive learning experiences, such as coding games or robotics projects, they develop strong analytical thinking abilities which contribute to their overall cognitive growth.

Exploring the Impact of Early AI Education on Black Children's Creativity

Exploring the impact of early exposure to AI education on the creativity of young individuals from marginalized communities offers valuable insights into their cognitive growth and innovative potential. Research suggests that providing black children with access to AI education at an early age can significantly enhance their creative abilities.

Creativity is a fundamental aspect of human cognition that plays a crucial role in problem-solving, critical thinking, and innovation. It involves the generation of novel ideas, products, or solutions. Early exposure to AI education can foster creativity in black children by introducing them to new technologies and computational thinking concepts. This exposure provides them with opportunities to explore different ways of thinking, conceptualize abstract ideas, and develop their imaginative skills.

Moreover, engaging black children in AI education from an early age allows them to experiment with various domains such as art, music, storytelling, and game design. These activities encourage divergent thinking and enable young learners to express themselves creatively through technology-based platforms. By nurturing their creativity through AI education, black children gain confidence in their unique perspectives and abilities.

Furthermore, fostering creativity among marginalized communities has broader societal implications. By empowering young individuals from these communities with AI education tools and knowledge, we not only promote inclusivity but also tap into previously untapped talent pools. The diverse perspectives and creative contributions of black individuals can enrich the field of artificial intelligence itself while addressing long-standing disparities in representation within this domain.

Addressing the Opportunity Gap: Early AI Education for Black Children

Addressing the opportunity gap for marginalized communities involves providing equitable access to educational resources that foster cognitive growth and innovative potential. Specifically, when considering early AI education for black children, several key factors come into play:

1. Curriculum: Designing a curriculum that incorporates relevant AI concepts and applications while being culturally responsive is crucial. This ensures that black children can see themselves reflected in the material, fostering a sense of belonging and engagement.
2. Qualified Educators: Hiring qualified educators who are not only well-versed in AI but also possess cultural competence is essential. These educators can effectively create inclusive learning environments where black children feel valued and supported.
3. Technological Infrastructure: Providing access to necessary technological infrastructure, such as computers and internet connectivity, is vital for ensuring all black children have equal opportunities to engage with AI education.
4. Partnerships: Collaborating with community organizations, academic institutions, and industry professionals can enhance the impact of early AI education for black children by facilitating mentorship programs, internships, and real-world applications of AI concepts.

Empowering Black Children through Early AI Education

Facilitating equitable access to AI resources and fostering inclusive learning environments can empower marginalized communities, particularly black children, by providing them with the tools and opportunities necessary for their cognitive growth and innovative potential.

Early AI education offers a platform for black children to develop critical thinking skills, problem-solving abilities, and computational thinking. By introducing AI concepts at an early age, these children are exposed to technological advancements that are shaping various industries worldwide.

Equitable access to AI resources ensures that black children have equal opportunities in acquiring knowledge about emerging technologies. This access allows them to explore AI applications such as machine learning algorithms or natural language processing, which have the potential to transform society in multiple domains.

Furthermore, inclusive learning environments promote a sense of belonging among black children within the field of AI education. Creating spaces where they feel welcome and supported fosters their confidence in pursuing careers related to artificial intelligence. Encouraging their participation also helps challenge prevailing stereotypes about who can excel in technical fields.

Empowering black children through early AI education not only serves as a means of addressing educational disparities but also has broader societal implications. By equipping them with the necessary skills and knowledge, we enable these individuals to actively contribute toward innovation, economic growth, and social progress while ensuring their rightful place within an increasingly technology-driven world.

Frequently Asked Questions

What Are Some Potential Challenges or Barriers to Implementing Early AI Education for Black Children?

Potential challenges and barriers to implementing early AI education for black children may include lack of access to resources, unequal distribution of educational opportunities, systemic discrimination in schools, and limited representation of black individuals in the field of AI.

How Can Early AI Education Specifically Benefit Black Children's Social and Emotional Development?

Early AI education has the potential to benefit black children's social and emotional development by providing opportunities for critical thinking, problem-solving, and creativity. This can enhance their self-confidence, communication skills, and ability to navigate an increasingly technologically driven world.

Are There Any Studies or Research That Demonstrate the Long-Term Impact of Early AI Education on Black Children's Academic Success?

Several studies and research have explored the long-term impact of early AI education on academic success for black children. These findings provide evidence of the positive effects that early AI education can have on their educational outcomes.

What Resources or Support Systems Are Available to Parents and Educators to Help Them Navigate Early AI Education for Black Children?

Resources and support systems available to parents and educators for navigating early AI education for black children include online platforms, workshops, and community organizations. These provide guidance in curriculum selection, teaching strategies, and fostering inclusivity in AI education.

How Can Early AI Education Help Black Children Develop Critical Thinking and Problem-Solving Skills for Future Career Opportunities?

Early AI education can aid in the development of critical thinking and problem-solving skills for future career opportunities. This knowledge equips black children with essential skills needed to navigate the increasingly technology-driven world.

Conclusion

In conclusion, early AI education for black children is not just a luxury but a necessity. It has the potential to revolutionize their cognitive skills, unleash their creativity, and bridge the opportunity gap.

By introducing them to AI at an early age, we are empowering these young minds to become future innovators and leaders. The benefits of early AI education cannot be overstated; it is a game-changer that will shape the trajectory of black children's development and propel them towards limitless possibilities.

Take Action by Supporting AI Education Initiatives and Advocating for Diversity in Tech

In today's rapidly evolving technological landscape, it is crucial to foster an environment that promotes inclusive and diverse perspectives in the field of AI education.

This section aims to shed light on the importance of supporting AI education initiatives and advocating for diversity within the tech industry.

By exploring the impact of AI education on future careers and addressing existing disparities in gender representation, this section provides strategies for encouraging individuals, particularly girls and women, to pursue tech education.

Ultimately, readers will gain insights into how they can actively contribute towards enhancing AI education and fostering diversity within the tech sector.

Key Takeaways

- Supporting AI education initiatives and advocating for diversity in tech fosters the development and dissemination of knowledge in the rapidly evolving field.
- Encouraging diverse hiring practices, implementing diversity training programs, and establishing partnerships with educational institutions focusing on underrepresented communities are effective strategies for advocating for diversity in the tech industry.
- AI education equips individuals with necessary skills and understanding, allowing them to thrive in the evolving job market and shape the future of AI while ensuring the responsible development and deployment of AI technologies.
- To encourage girls and women to pursue tech education, mentorship programs, challenging stereotypes and biases, showcasing successful role models, and fostering confidence and motivation are important strategies.

The Importance of Supporting AI Education Initiatives

Supporting AI education initiatives is crucial for fostering the development and dissemination of knowledge in this rapidly evolving field. As artificial intelligence (AI) continues to advance and permeate various industries, it becomes increasingly important to equip individuals with the necessary skills and understanding to navigate this complex landscape. By investing in AI education initiatives, society can ensure that a diverse range of individuals have access to opportunities for learning, growth, and innovation.

AI education initiatives provide a platform for individuals from diverse backgrounds to engage with AI technologies, theories, and applications. This inclusivity is essential for fostering a sense of belonging within the AI community. It allows people from different ethnicities, genders, socioeconomic backgrounds, and educational levels to participate actively in shaping the future of AI.

Moreover, supporting these initiatives enables the dissemination of knowledge across different sectors. By providing accessible resources and training programs, we can empower individuals who may not have traditional academic backgrounds or financial means to contribute meaningfully to the field. This democratization of AI education ensures that valuable perspectives are not overlooked due to systemic barriers.

Ways to Advocate for Diversity in the Tech Industry

Promoting inclusivity and representation within the technology industry can be achieved through various strategies.

One effective way to advocate for diversity in the tech industry is by creating and supporting mentorship programs. These programs provide opportunities for underrepresented individuals to connect with experienced professionals who can offer guidance, support, and insights into navigating the industry.

Additionally, advocating for diverse hiring practices is crucial in promoting inclusivity. Encouraging companies to adopt policies that actively seek out candidates from diverse backgrounds helps ensure a more inclusive workforce.

Another strategy is fostering an inclusive workplace culture by implementing diversity training programs and workshops that educate employees on unconscious bias, cultural sensitivity, and inclusivity. This helps create an environment where all individuals feel valued, respected, and included.

Furthermore, establishing partnerships with educational institutions or organizations that focus on underrepresented communities can also promote diversity in the tech industry. By providing resources, scholarships, or internships specifically targeting these groups, access to opportunities within the field becomes more equitable.

Lastly, hosting events or conferences centered around diversity in technology serves as platforms for networking and knowledge sharing among professionals from different backgrounds. These events not only showcase diverse talent but also provide opportunities for collaboration and growth.

The Impact of AI Education on Future Careers

The impact of AI education on future careers can be seen in the increased demand for professionals with expertise in artificial intelligence and machine learning. As technology continues to advance, industries are recognizing the need for individuals who possess the skills and knowledge to develop and implement AI systems. This growing demand is evident across various sectors, including healthcare, finance, manufacturing, and transportation.

Professionals with a strong foundation in AI education are well-positioned to thrive in this evolving job market. They have the ability to design intelligent algorithms, analyze complex data sets, and develop innovative solutions that can enhance efficiency and productivity within organizations. Furthermore, individuals with expertise in AI are sought after for their ability to leverage machine learning techniques to automate processes, predict trends, and make data-driven decisions.

Moreover, as AI becomes increasingly integrated into everyday life, there is a need for professionals who not only possess technical skills but also understand the ethical implications of AI technologies. This includes considerations such as bias mitigation, privacy protection, and transparency in decision-making processes. Thus, by investing in AI education and developing a diverse workforce that reflects different perspectives and experiences, organizations can ensure responsible development and deployment of AI technologies.

Strategies for Encouraging Girls and Women to Pursue Tech Education

One effective strategy for increasing the representation of girls and women in tech education is to provide mentorship programs that connect aspiring female students with successful women already working in the industry. Mentorship programs have been recognized as a valuable tool for empowering and encouraging underrepresented groups, such as girls and women, to pursue careers in technology. These programs create opportunities for aspiring female students to receive guidance, support, and advice from experienced professionals who have navigated the challenges of the tech industry.

By connecting aspiring female students with successful women already working in the industry, mentorship programs offer a sense of belonging and community. They provide a platform for sharing experiences, discussing career goals, and developing professional networks. This support system fosters confidence and motivation among young women interested in pursuing tech education.

Moreover, mentorship programs help address gender disparities by challenging stereotypes and biases associated with females' capabilities in technology-related fields. By showcasing successful role models who have achieved significant accomplishments within the industry, these programs inspire aspiring female students to believe in their own potential.

Addressing the Lack of Diversity in AI and Tech Fields

Addressing the lack of diversity in AI and tech fields requires implementing comprehensive strategies that aim to dismantle structural barriers and promote equal opportunities for underrepresented groups. The current state of diversity in these fields is characterized by an underrepresentation of women, racial and ethnic minorities, individuals from lower socioeconomic backgrounds, and people with disabilities. This lack of diversity not only hinders the advancement of marginalized groups but also limits innovation and perpetuates inequalities.

To address this issue, it is crucial to establish inclusive hiring practices that actively seek out diverse candidates. Additionally, creating mentorship programs, scholarships, and internships specifically targeted at underrepresented groups can provide them with opportunities to gain experience and develop their skills in AI and tech fields. Promoting outreach initiatives in schools and communities can spark interest among younger generations who may otherwise be unaware of the possibilities within these industries.

Furthermore, fostering a culture of inclusivity within organizations is essential for attracting and retaining diverse talent. This involves creating safe spaces where individuals feel empowered to share their perspectives without fear of discrimination or bias. Providing ongoing training on diversity awareness can also help combat unconscious bias and ensure fair treatment for all employees.

How Readers Can Make a Difference in AI Education and Tech Diversity

Promoting awareness and engagement with efforts aiming to enhance diversity in AI education and the tech industry can contribute to meaningful change. There are several ways readers can make a difference in AI education and advocate for diversity in the tech field:

- Support organizations and initiatives that prioritize diversity and inclusion in AI education, such as Girls Who Code or Black Girls Code.
- Encourage educational institutions to offer more diverse and inclusive curricula that highlight the contributions of underrepresented groups in AI.
- Participate in mentorship programs or volunteer opportunities that connect individuals

from underrepresented backgrounds with opportunities in AI education and the tech industry.

- Advocate for policies and practices that promote diversity, such as implementing blind recruitment processes or establishing diversity targets within companies.
- Engage with online communities, forums, and conferences dedicated to discussing diversity issues within AI education and the tech industry.

By actively participating in these actions, readers can help create an environment where everyone feels welcomed, valued, and included. This collective effort towards enhancing diversity will not only benefit individuals from underrepresented groups but also foster innovation by bringing together diverse perspectives.

Together we can build a more inclusive future for AI education and the tech industry.

Frequently Asked Questions

What Are Some Specific AI Education Initiatives That Readers Can Support?

There are several specific AI education initiatives available for support, such as providing access to online courses, establishing AI-focused educational programs in schools, and funding scholarships for underrepresented individuals pursuing AI education.

How Can Individuals Advocate for Diversity in the Tech Industry on a Personal Level?

Advocating for diversity in the tech industry on a personal level involves promoting inclusive practices, challenging biases, and fostering an environment that values diverse perspectives. This can contribute to a more equitable and innovative tech sector.

What Are Some Potential Career Opportunities for Individuals Who Pursue AI Education?

Potential career opportunities for individuals who pursue AI education include roles such as data scientists, machine learning engineers, research scientists, and AI consultants. These professionals can contribute to various industries by developing innovative solutions and advancing the field of artificial intelligence.

Are There Any Specific Strategies or Programs in Place to Encourage Girls and Women to Pursue Tech Education?

Efforts to encourage girls and women to pursue tech education include various strategies and programs. These initiatives aim to address the gender gap in the field and provide opportunities for underrepresented groups to develop skills in technology-related fields.

What Are Some Underlying Reasons for the Lack of Diversity in AI and Tech Fields, and How Can They Be Addressed?

The lack of diversity in AI and tech fields can be attributed to factors such as unconscious bias, gender stereotypes, and limited access to resources. Addressing these issues requires promoting inclusive policies, providing equal opportunities, and fostering a supportive environment for underrepresented groups.

Conclusion

In conclusion, supporting AI education initiatives and advocating for diversity in the tech industry is like nurturing a garden of possibilities. By empowering young minds with knowledge and skills in AI, we are sowing seeds that will blossom into future careers filled with innovation and progress.

Encouraging girls and women to pursue tech education is akin to unlocking a hidden treasure trove of untapped potential. Together, by addressing the lack of diversity in AI and tech fields, we can cultivate a vibrant ecosystem where everyone thrives.

Let us join hands to make a difference in AI education and tech diversity, creating a brighter tomorrow for all.

An Optimistic Outlook on the Positive Changes That Widespread AI Education for Black Children Can Bring to Society

One potential objection to the widespread AI education for black children is the concern that it may perpetuate existing educational inequalities. However, this section aims to present an optimistic outlook on the positive changes that such education can bring to society.

By empowering black children through AI education, breaking stereotypes, and fostering social equality, we argue that AI education has the potential to transform both individual lives and society as a whole.

This section explores the impact of widespread AI education for black children and its implications for a more inclusive and equitable future.

Key Takeaways

- AI education addresses disparities in educational systems, particularly for marginalized communities like Black children.
- AI education provides personalized learning experiences catering to individual strengths and weaknesses.
- AI education paves the way for increased academic achievement and future success.
- AI education helps bridge gaps in economic mobility and improve social equity.

The Power of AI Education in Bridging the Racial Education Gap

The potential impact of AI education in addressing the racial education gap is a topic of considerable interest and importance. In recent years, there has been growing recognition of the disparities that exist within educational systems, particularly for marginalized communities such as Black children. AI education offers a promising solution to bridge this gap and create more equitable opportunities for all students.

One way in which AI education can address the racial education gap is by providing personalized learning experiences. Traditional educational approaches often fail to meet the diverse needs of students, resulting in unequal outcomes. However, AI technology has the ability to adapt and tailor instruction based on individual strengths, weaknesses, and learning styles. By utilizing data-driven algorithms and machine learning techniques, AI can provide targeted support and interventions that are specifically designed to meet each student's unique needs.

Furthermore, AI education can also help overcome systemic biases that perpetuate inequality in traditional classrooms. Research has shown that teachers may have unconscious biases that affect their expectations and evaluations of students from different racial backgrounds. By relying on objective algorithms rather than human judgment alone, AI education can help mitigate these biases and ensure fair treatment for all students.

Empowering Black Children through AI Education

Empowering black children through the implementation of AI educational programs has the potential to foster equal opportunities for growth and development. By harnessing the power of artificial intelligence, these programs can address the unique needs and challenges faced by black children in their educational journey.

AI education can provide personalized learning experiences that cater to individual strengths and weaknesses, allowing students to progress at their own pace.

One key benefit of AI education is its ability to mitigate biases that may exist within traditional teaching methods. By relying on algorithms and data analysis, AI systems can minimize human biases and ensure fair treatment for all learners. This is particularly crucial in creating an inclusive environment where black children feel valued and supported.

Moreover, AI educational programs offer a wide range of resources that may not be readily available in underserved communities. With access to quality content, interactive tools, and virtual mentors, black children can expand their knowledge base beyond what is offered within their immediate surroundings. This exposure paves the way for increased academic achievement and future success.

Breaking Stereotypes: AI Education and Black Children's Potential

Breaking stereotypes in AI education for black children necessitates an examination of the potential barriers that hinder their academic progress and a proactive effort to address those obstacles. By identifying and addressing these barriers, we can create an inclusive learning environment that allows black children to thrive in AI education.

To understand the potential barriers, it is important to consider various factors:

- Socioeconomic Challenges:
- Limited access to resources such as computers or high-speed internet.
- Lack of financial means to afford AI-related courses or programs.
- Cultural Stereotypes:
- Negative stereotypes that suggest AI is not a suitable field for black individuals.
- Underrepresentation of black professionals in AI fields, leading to a lack of role models and encouragement.

Efforts must be made to overcome these barriers and provide support for black children in AI education:

- Equal Access Initiatives:
- Providing affordable or free access to necessary technology and resources.
- Offering scholarships or funding opportunities specifically targeted at black students.
- Representation and Mentoring Programs:
- Promoting diversity by actively recruiting black educators and professionals in the field.
- Establishing mentorship programs where successful black individuals can guide aspiring students.

AI Education as a Catalyst for Social Equality

AI education has the potential to foster social equality by providing equal opportunities for marginalized communities to access and excel in technology-related fields. By offering comprehensive and inclusive AI education programs, society can address the existing disparities that hinder marginalized communities' participation in technology-related fields. Accessible AI education can empower individuals from these communities to acquire the skills and knowledge needed to engage with emerging technologies, thereby breaking down barriers to entry into high-demand industries.

The implementation of AI education initiatives can help bridge gaps in economic mobility and improve social equity. Historically, marginalized communities have faced limited access to educational resources and opportunities due to various socioeconomic factors. However, with the expansion of AI education programs, individuals from these communities can gain access to quality instruction and training that prepares them for careers in technology. This increased accessibility creates a more level playing field and reduces systemic biases that perpetuate inequality.

Moreover, AI education fosters a sense of belonging by creating spaces where individuals from marginalized communities feel valued and included. By recognizing their unique perspectives and contributions, AI education promotes diversity within the technology sector—diversity that is crucial for innovation and problem-solving. Through inclusive educational environments, marginalized individuals are empowered to express themselves freely without fear of judgment or exclusion.

The Future Is Now: AI Education for Black Children

One potential area of focus for future research on AI education could be the exploration of strategies and approaches to effectively engage and support Black children in acquiring AI-related skills. This is an important consideration as it has been widely recognized that there are existing disparities in access to quality education and resources for marginalized communities, including Black children. By addressing this gap, society can work towards creating a more inclusive and equitable future, where all individuals have equal opportunities to participate in and benefit from advancements in AI technology.

To effectively engage and support Black children in acquiring AI-related skills, research could explore the following strategies:

- Culturally responsive teaching: Tailoring educational content and approaches to reflect the cultural backgrounds and experiences of Black children.
- Mentorship programs: Providing opportunities for Black students to connect with mentors who can provide guidance, support, and encouragement throughout their AI learning journey.

Transforming Society: The Impact of Widespread AI Education for Black Children

The previous subtopic discussed the potential of AI education for black children. In this section, we will shift our focus to the broader impact that widespread AI education for black children can have on society.

The transformation of society through widespread AI education for black children is a significant area of research and policy interest. By providing access to quality AI education, we can empower black children to develop critical skills needed in an increasingly digital world. This access not only bridges the educational divide but also addresses systemic inequalities that have historically disadvantaged black communities.

With widespread AI education, black children can acquire essential technical competencies and knowledge required for future employment opportunities in emerging fields such as data science and artificial intelligence. Equipping them with these skills enhances their social mobility and economic prospects, enabling them to contribute meaningfully to society.

Moreover, increased representation of black individuals in tech-related fields can lead to the development of culturally relevant technologies that address specific societal challenges faced by marginalized communities. By diversifying perspectives within the field of AI, we foster innovation and ensure equitable outcomes for all members of society.

Overall, the positive impact of widespread AI education for black children extends beyond personal empowerment; it has the potential to transform society by dismantling barriers and promoting inclusivity in various spheres.

Frequently Asked Questions

How Does AI Education Specifically Address the Racial Education Gap?

AI education specifically addresses the racial education gap by providing equal access to educational resources and opportunities. Through personalized learning, adaptive algorithms, and targeted interventions, AI can help bridge the achievement disparities among black children and contribute to a more equitable society.

What Are Some Examples of AI Education Programs That Have Successfully Empowered Black Children?

Examples of successful AI education programs empowering black children include initiatives that provide access to quality educational resources, personalized learning experiences, and mentorship opportunities. These programs aim to bridge the racial education gap and foster academic achievement among disadvantaged students.

How Does AI Education Challenge and Break Stereotypes Surrounding Black Children's Potential?

AI education challenges and breaks stereotypes surrounding the potential of black children. Research shows that AI-based learning platforms have improved academic performance, increased self-confidence, and fostered a sense of belonging among black students.

Can You Provide Specific Examples of How AI Education Has Contributed to Social Equality?

AI education has contributed to social equality by providing equal access to educational resources and opportunities for marginalized communities. It has helped bridge the digital divide, promote inclusivity, and empower individuals from diverse backgrounds to thrive in the digital age.

What Are the Potential Long-Term Effects of Widespread AI Education for Black Children on Society as a Whole?

The potential long-term effects of widespread AI education for black children on society as a whole may include increased access to opportunities, improved social mobility, enhanced economic growth, and reduced educational disparities.

Conclusion

In conclusion, the widespread education of black children in AI holds immense potential for positive change in society. By bridging the racial education gap, AI education empowers these children and breaks stereotypes, revealing their true potential.

Furthermore, it serves as a catalyst for social equality, paving the way towards a more inclusive future. The impact of this transformative education is already being felt, with society reaping the benefits of diverse perspectives and innovative solutions.

With AI education for black children, we are witnessing the dawn of a new era that promises a brighter and more equitable future for all.

BOOKS BY THIS AUTHOR

Hidden In Plain Sight: The Legacy Of Slavery

ASIN : B0C87F9GV7

As young people coming of age in the 21st century, we've all heard about 'the talk' that our parents have with us. But for Black kids, there's a different kind of talk: one where we're taught to be aware of our surroundings at all times and how to protect ourselves from potential danger.
This book is a collection of easily verifiable topics of conversation. I am neither a scholar nor a historian, so I strongly recommend that you and your children do your own research; only then will they truly understand the rules of engagement.

Ai, Race, And Discrimination: Confronting Racial Bias In Artificial Intelligence

ASIN : B0CHCP31ND

From biased hiring processes to skewed criminal justice systems, the impact of AI-driven discrimination is far-reaching and profoundly damaging
As artificial intelligence becomes an integral part of our lives, its inherent biases are proving to be more insidious than anticipated, magnifying the very inequalities it was meant to address.

I Hate My Job: A Journal For Documenting Workplace Discrimination And Harassment

ASIN : B0CDNPT4T7

Employees have the right to work in an environment free from discrimination and harassment, and employers have a responsibility to prevent and address this behavior in the workplace.

www.ingramcontent.com/pod-product-compliance
Lightning Source LLC
LaVergne TN
LVHW081757050326
832903LV00027B/1982